SECTION B
Planning

Effective practice depends on many factors, not the least of which is proper planning and preparation

Other Books in the Group Work Practice Kit

Effective Planning for Groups

Effective Planning for Groups

Janice L. DeLucia-Waack
University at Buffalo,
State University of New York

Amy Nitza
Indiana University–Purdue
University Fort Wayne

Los Angeles | London | New Delhi
Singapore | Washington DC

Los Angeles | London | New Delhi
Singapore | Washington DC

FOR INFORMATION:

SAGE Publications, Inc.
2455 Teller Road
Thousand Oaks, California 91320
E-mail: order@sagepub.com

SAGE Publications Ltd.
1 Oliver's Yard
55 City Road
London EC1Y 1SP
United Kingdom

SAGE Publications India Pvt. Ltd.
B 1/I 1 Mohan Cooperative Industrial Area
Mathura Road, New Delhi 110 044
India

SAGE Publications Asia-Pacific Pte. Ltd.
3 Church Street
#10-04 Samsung Hub
Singapore 049483

Copyright © 2014 by SAGE Publications, Inc.

All rights reserved. No part of this book may be reproduced or utilized in any form or by any means, electronic or mechanical, including photocopying, recording, or by any information storage and retrieval system, without permission in writing from the publisher.

Printed in the United States of America

Library of Congress Cataloging-in-Publication Data

A catalog record of this book is available from the Library of Congress.

9781483332307

This book is printed on acid-free paper.

Acquisitions Editor: Kassie Graves
Editorial Assistant: Elizabeth Luizzi
Production Editor: Brittany Bauhaus
Copy Editor: Megan Granger
Typesetter: C&M Digitals (P) Ltd.
Proofreader: Rae-Ann Goodwin
Indexer: Marilyn Augst
Cover Designer: Anupama Krishnan
Marketing Manager: Shari Countryman

13 14 15 16 17 10 9 8 7 6 5 4 3 2 1

Brief Contents _____

_____ Detailed Contents

1

Introduction

Current best practice (Thomas & Pender, 2008) suggests that groups are essentially designed and planned before the first group member is interviewed. In practice, however, this is often not the case. In fact, popular myth suggests that planning somehow signifies incompetence. Bob Conyne (1999) said it best in *Failures in Group Work: How We Can Learn From Our Mistakes*: "In fact, not so long ago, it was believed by many (some to this day) that if group leaders were 'really good,' not only did they not need to plan but the planning would distract from their spontaneity and effectiveness as group leaders" (p. 8).

In contrast, the Association for Specialists in Group Work (ASGW) *Best Practice Guidelines* (Thomas & Pender, 2008) suggests three major emphases in best practice for groups: planning, performing, and processing. Planning is essential to effective group leadership. Planning often takes as much time and energy as, sometimes even more than, the actual group leadership. Good planning ensures that group members have been carefully selected and prepared for group, group goals match individual goals, group interventions have been selected to meet group goals, and coleaders have a good working relationship and an agreed-on plan for the group.

Planning is different depending on the type of group, but each group requires substantial planning time. Task groups involve people who come together for a common goal; group supervision, planning meetings, clubs, task forces, staff development, community presentations, and classrooms are all examples of task groups. For a task group, much of the planning time may be spent on an ecological assessment where leaders listen to their community and see what the needs are. For example, a school principal might decide that an ecology club is needed. Focused discussion with teachers would indicate those teachers who are willing to act as advisors to such a club and who have expertise and interest in land and water conservation and in ways to leave less of a carbon footprint. Discussions with students would indicate whether land and water conservation are of interest to them. Discussion with the local community agencies would indicate whether there was need for a campaign and interventions around water conservation and water pollution. If so, the club advisor might decide to partner with the local water conservation council to create public service announcements and volunteer on a local water conservation project. The ecological assessment is the major focus for a task group and leads into goals and activities of the group. The teacher advisor would also have to create a schedule and familiarize him or herself with the guidelines of how to lead an effective task group (Thomas & Pender, 2008; Wilson, Rapin, & Haley-Banez, 2000). DeLucia-Waack and Nitza (2011) provided suggestions for leading task groups, as well as specific guidelines for task groups in schools (DeLucia-Waack & Nitza, 2010).

For psychoeducational groups, once the goals of the group have been decided based on the needs of potential group members, group leaders need to spend time reviewing the current literature on group practice and research to identify resources and group interventions that will be helpful as they plan the group. Case examples are provided in Chapter 7 and throughout this book. For help in planning psychoeducational groups, see Bauman and Steen (2010, 2012); DeLucia-Waack (2006); DeLucia-Waack, Bridbord, Kleiner, and Nitza (2006); DeLucia-Waack, Segrist, and Horne (2008); Foss, Green, Wolfe-Stiltner, & DeLucia-Waack (2008); Morganett (1990, 1994); Salazar (2009); and Smead (1995, 1996).

MacGowan and Hanbidge (2013) provide an excellent example of planning for an evidence-based counseling group:

Rosa Gutiérrez is a newly hired group worker at a community mental health center (CMHC) located in a large metropolitan area. She recently graduated with a master's degree in social work and had brief previous experience working at another CMHC. She is fully bilingual and considers herself a bicultural Latina, the population mostly served by the center. Rosa was asked to lead a group for Latinas diagnosed with depression and without medical insurance. To fulfill her mandate, Rosa felt she needed to get a better idea of the best available evidence for providing services that were culturally responsive to depressed Latina groups. Her supervisor's limited knowledge about evidence-based practices caused Rosa some initial concern; however, she recommended that Rosa speak with a field instructor who had access to relevant, summarized literature located in peer-reviewed journals. At a team meeting, Rosa advocated for and was supported by the organization in the development of a new evidence-based group work (EBGW) intervention. A Spanish-speaking bilingual staff member named Maria, who was knowledgeable about evidence-based practice, volunteered to cofacilitate the Latina depression group with Rosa.

To begin the EBGW process, Rosa formulated a question: In establishing a culturally relevant group for Latinas, what relatively brief (10–12 sessions) group intervention will best reduce depression? Evidence was collected from the literature to see if there was an effective group approach for low-income Latinas or if a mainstream option would need to be adapted. Group treatments for depression, primarily using cognitive behavioral and interpersonal therapy, had been rated as "well established" for adolescents and adults (Johnson, 2008; Levy & O'Hara, 2010, cf. Table 1). Other culturally appropriate material (Muñoz, Ippen, Rao, Le, & Dwyer, 2000; Muñoz & Mendelson, 2005; Muñoz & Miranda, 1986) was identified, without the need for substantial modifications. Rosa and Maria critically appraised the evidence for its rigor, impact, and applicability, and then applied the evidence to address Rosa's question. They related the three areas of rigor, impact, and applicability to Bond, Drake, and Becker's (2010) nine "ideal features" of a mental health intervention and decided to implement the cognitive behavioral group therapy model, as it was developed specifically for low-income Latino/as. They utilized the 12-week model, which included the core elements of the intervention but not the extra 4-week module related to health issues, as it was not deemed relevant (Muñoz & Miranda, 1986). The manual was available electronically in Spanish and English (Muñoz et al., 2000). Rosa and Maria also included discussion about challenges in the acculturation process, which may contribute to depressive symptoms (Levy & O'Hara, 2010), included group content that recognized acculturation as a bidirectional process, and addressed acculturation issues related to gender (e.g., mother and child challenges, financial stressors). Group sessions would also include information about accessing no-cost community resources.

In terms of process, Rosa and Maria reviewed the American Group Psychotherapy Association (AGPA, 2007) and Association for the Advancement of Social Work with Groups (2005) practice standards and the ASGW diversity competence principles (Singh, Merchant, Skudrzyk, & Ingene, 2012) to prepare and implement the intervention. Specifically, ethnically and linguistically matched therapists offering the group in client-preferred languages is important and improves outcomes (Smith, Rodríguez, & Bernal, 2011). It is also important to explicitly emphasize the cultural values of the clients throughout group sessions (Griner & Smith, 2006). Rosa would also selectively disclose personal information to enhance a personalized professional relationship with group members that would help build the therapeutic alliance, reflecting *personalismo*, or value for the personal connection in relationships. In addition, they would monitor how the group received the material.

To secure referrals, Rosa shared information with the local hospital's family health clinic, noting that transportation vouchers would be offered (Stacciarini, O'Keeffe, & Mathews, 2007). The Group Selection Questionnaire (Burlingame, Cox, Davies, Layne, & Gleave, 2011) was administered to select group members. Additionally, to maximize cohesion, the maximum number of group members would be set at nine. Group orientation sessions were arranged so prospective group members could meet Rosa and Maria over coffee and pastries, with specific information about the group shared in those sessions (AGPA, 2007). They discussed handouts (in Spanish) that oriented group members to the group experience. For an outcome measure, the Patient Health Questionnaire (PHQ–9; available in English and Spanish) was used to measures both depression symptoms and their severity (Martin, Rief, Klaiberg, & Braehler, 2006). The PHQ–9 was selected because it is brief, easy to administer, and free of charge (available at www.integration.samhsa.gov/images/res/PHQ%20-%20Questions.pdf). Depression scores would be measured every couple of weeks and charted over time. In addition, group members would complete a brief evaluation of each session (Rose, 1984), which would ask them to rate on a scale from 1 (not at all) to 5 (very highly satisfied), "How satisfied were you with today's session?" (in Spanish), and to comment if they wished. These ratings would be reviewed weekly. To assess cohesion, the Group Psychotherapy Intervention Rating Scale (GPIRS) was used (Chapman, Baker, Porter, Thayer, & Burlingame, 2010).

At the end of the group sessions, Rosa and Maria reviewed both the outcomes and process of the group. Reflecting on the MAP (Member-relevant, Answerable, Practice question). question, the main purpose of the group was to reduce depression. She and Maria reviewed the depression progress chart, member satisfaction scores, and ratings from the GPIRS to determine group effectiveness and cohesion. Process and outcome results were communicated with the agency team to determine the implications for offering another Latina depression group.

The ASGW *Best Practice Guidelines* (Thomas & Pender, 2008) delineate the following steps as part of the planning process:

- Assessment of values and skills related to type of group
- Ecological assessment
- Group development and design

  o Type of group and how it meets community needs
  o Purpose and goals of group
  o Fees, schedule, and meeting place (unique accommodations based on population)
  o Techniques and leadership style

    - Activities and group plans from the literature
    - Adaptation from literature and empirically supported treatments to this group population

  o Recruitment materials
  o Screening and selection criteria and outline

    - Professional disclosure statement
    - Procedures for informed consent
    - Information about confidentiality (and limits of)

  o Preparation materials
  o Evaluation measures (outcome and process)

This book is designed to lead readers through the specific steps of designing and planning a group, focusing on psychoeducational and counseling/therapy groups. A specific outline will be provided sequentially as a guide for the planning process. Included will be suggestions about how to select, organize, and arrange activities, as well as relevant resources. Important topics to be discussed in this book include pregroup decision making based on the goals and population of the group, selection of interventions, securing agency and school support, recruitment strategies, selection criteria, leadership preparation, and supervision.

There are several good reasons why group leaders often skip one or more of these vital steps in the planning process. Long before the group starts, several important decisions need to be made about the structure, content, and interventions to be used. However, these decisions cannot be made in a vacuum; information must be gathered about what has been shown to be effective, the setting, and potential participants' needs and interests.

Purpose of the Book

Any intentional group is based on a coherent group plan. This book will identify the elements that are basic to any plan and will apply these elements within an ongoing example. The following chapters focus on identification of a population, type of group, and group goals; rationale for using groups; procedural decisions based on best practices; leader preparation; planning group sessions; and case examples.

2

What Type of Group for Whom With What Goals?

Identification of a Target Population, Type of Group, and Group Goals

Planning for a group involves several steps. The first and arguably most important, as it determines the content and procedures of all other steps, is identification of a target population and subsequent identification of type of group and group goals. Once the target population and the type of group are identified, goals should be easily identifiable. This chapter leads you through these key steps with illustrative examples.

Identification of a Population

This decision comes from the setting where you work and the people with whom you work. Who are your clients or potential group members? Are they students in your school, clients in your agency or work setting, or possibly colleagues for whom you have been asked to provide training and/or supervision? Once you decide who will be the recipient of the group intervention, you can begin to work on the type of group and goals based on what is needed.

Needs and Environmental Assessment

A needs assessment is the first step in the gathering of essential information to plan a group. There are several ways to do this. One is to ask potential group members. In the schools, even elementary schools, students can be provided with a list of potential group topics and asked to indicate which, if any, groups they would like to participate in. Experience in schools suggests that it is helpful to ask students not only what groups they would be interested in but also what groups other students might find useful. In an agency or other settings, clients may be asked about what groups they would perceive as helpful and/or be willing to participate in.

Staff who work with potential group members are also a valuable source of information about what kinds of groups would be useful. In schools, parents and teachers can provide a suggested list of helpful group topics. Additionally, counselors in the schools and community agencies who are working with clients individually are a good source of information about groups that would be appropriate. Once data have been collected using a survey and/or staff and counselor input, group leaders may then begin to decide what groups are most needed at this time. For example, parents may suggest that students need a school survival group that focuses on time management and organizational skills. Teachers might suggest that students need a coping skills group to manage stress. In an agency, counselors might suggest a psychoeducational group that focuses on teaching basic communication skills and also a counseling group that helps group members identify and change the attitudes, feelings, and behaviors that are currently causing problems in their relationships.

Choosing a Type of Group

The next step in the design of a group plan is to determine what type of group may be the most appropriate and effective to address the identified needs. The Association for Specialists in Group Work (ASGW) classifies three different categories of groups focused on individual growth and change: psychoeducational, counseling, and therapy groups (Wilson, Rapin, & Haley-Banez, 2000). While there is overlap among these types of groups, they each emphasize different types of goals and mechanisms for achieving those goals.

Psychoeducational groups promote the development of skills and coping strategies, and provide information and opportunities for practice. Psychoeducational interventions assist group members in sharing and developing improved ways of functioning to deal with new or difficult situations; goals may be cognitive, affective, and/or behavioral. These groups generally emphasize learning through content and may use learning strategies to introduce and teach new skills, or to practice and strengthen existing skills. Psychoeducational groups teach specific skills and coping strategies in an effort to prevent problems (such as anger management, social skills, stress management, conflict resolution, assertiveness, cognitive restructuring). Relatedly, they tend to be more structured than other types of groups, with activities designed to facilitate discussion of a topic and/or development of new skills and behaviors. Psychoeducational groups also tend to be shorter in length—typically 4 to 14 sessions. Communication skills, coping skills, stress management, and managing emotions are examples of psychoeducational groups for all age groups and settings. Most groups in schools are psychoeducational, even if they are designed for a particular population or issue. For example, children-of-divorce groups in schools are typically designed to teach skills such as identification and communication of emotions, problem-solving and brainstorming coping strategies, and communication skills.

Counseling groups "address personal and interpersonal problems of living and promote personal and interpersonal growth and development" (Wilson et al., 2000, p. 331). While education and skill development can certainly occur, the emphasis is on interactions, mutual sharing, and emotional growth among group members. They use group process and dynamics to identify interpersonal difficulties, develop new ways of thinking and behaving, solve interpersonal problems, practice new behaviors, and learn coping skills from other group members. The major premise in counseling groups is that group members eventually act in a group as they behave in their relationships with others (significant others, friends, coworkers). Thus, as behaviors are enacted, group members can evaluate (with the help of other group members) the effectiveness of these behaviors (both positive and negative) on their relationships. A recent study (Bridbord & DeLucia-Waack, 2011) indicated a range of groups in practice: 72.2% therapy groups, 13% counseling groups, 11.19% psychoeducational groups, and 14.8% support groups.

Therapy groups "address personal and interpersonal problems of living, remediate perceptual and cognitive distortions or repetitive patterns of dysfunctional behavior, and promote personal and interpersonal growth and development" (Wilson et al., 2000, p. 331). Therapy groups are also heavily process oriented but focus more on remediation of problems that are chronic or severe in nature. Repetitive and dysfunctional patterns of thinking, behaving, and interacting with others are examined. Therapy groups tend to be longer in length and number of sessions, and may occur in residential or hospital settings.

Selecting among these types of groups involves considering the needs identified in a particular setting and identifying the emphasis that will be used to address those needs. For example, if a needs assessment in a school reveals a need for a group to support children with learning disabilities, both psychoeducational and counseling group formats may be appropriate. Both would offer universality and support for students struggling with this issue. However, a psychoeducational group might emphasize the development of improved study and test-taking skills (e.g., Steen, 2011), as well as the development of coping strategies for dealing with anger, frustration, or hopelessness. A counseling group might instead emphasize the social and relational difficulties associated with having a learning disability, including rejection, loneliness, and low self-esteem, as well as strained relationships with family members or authority figures. The emphasis in this group would be less on the development of new skills and more on the exploration and expression of feelings, reduction of tension and stress through self-disclosure, and receiving empathic support (Shechtman, 2007).

Identification of Group Goals

A group leader decides the general goals for the group prior to selection of group members, then tailors specific content and interventions once individual members of the group are identified. At this time, group leaders need to look at the current research and practice literature related to the group topics they have identified. Once a group topic is chosen, it is essential to utilize the most up-to-date resources that suggest a current theoretical understanding of the problem or need, specific group goals that are attainable, topics that are typically addressed in this type of group, and group interventions and activities focused on the topics that meet group goals. Current group counseling texts such as Sam Gladding's (2003) *Group Work: A Counseling Specialty* and Corey, Corey, and Corey's (2010) *Groups: Process and Practice* include chapter(s) specifically focused on groups for children and adolescents. The *Handbook of Group Counseling and Psychotherapy* (DeLucia-Waack, Kalodner, & Riva, 2013) has specific chapters on special topics and settings, integrating current research and practice. In addition, journals such as *Journal for Specialists in Group Work*; *Small Group Research*; *International Journal of Group Psychotherapy*; *Group Dynamics: Theory, Research, and Practice*; *Social Work with Groups*; *Journal of Counseling and Development*; *The Professional School Counselor*; *Journal of School Counseling*; *Journal of Child and Adolescent Group Therapy*; *Journal of Adolescence*; *Group*; *Journal of Group Psychotherapy, Psychodrama, and Sociometry*; *Journal of School Psychology*; *Psychology in the School*; *School Psychology Review*; *School Psychology Quarterly*; *Small Group Behavior*; *Special Services in the Schools*; *Adolescence*; *Child and Adolescent Social Work Journal*; *Child Development*; *Journal of Adolescent Health*; *Journal of Early Adolescence*; *Journal of Research on Adolescence*; *Journal of Youth and Adolescence*; and *New Directions for Child Development* provide cutting-edge information about current group research and practice.

For example, Sommers-Flanagan, Barrett-Hakanson, Clarke, and Sommers-Flanagan's (2000) article in *Journal for Specialists in Group Work* addresses psychoeducational school-based groups for depressed students, focusing on coping and social skills. Using a cognitive-behavioral framework, goals for treatment and corresponding group topics, group characteristics, and group interventions are described in a session-by-session format. Most issues of *Journal for Specialists in Group Work* include these kinds of articles.

Another helpful source of information about what groups are needed, what groups have typically worked, and what interventions have been most useful is practitioners in the field. School counselors should attend local school counseling meetings to talk to other school counselors who have led groups in their schools. Mental health counselors should talk to colleagues, as well as other professionals in the field. When one of the authors was designing interventions using music for children of divorce groups, the school counselors who piloted group sessions were helpful in two ways: First, they were clear that eight sessions for a children-of-divorce group was realistic, rather than the 20 proposed. Second, they were helpful in figuring out the order of sessions that worked best for students. There was a session titled "Is It My Fault?" that originally was planned as the second session. Several school counselors said that it was not working as the second session because the children were not ready to disclose such a personal fear so early on. Moving the session to later in the group made it much more effective because the children were more comfortable, and thus more willing to disclose their fears.

Once a range of possible group goals has been identified based on the current literature and practice, specific goals may then be chosen based on interviews with potential group members about their concerns, a formal assessment of member concerns, or group discussion and consensus of what issues the group should focus on. Interview and assessment procedures will be discussed in Book 7.

It is helpful for several reasons to write out the goals as a first step toward planning the group. First, all activities should be based on the specific goals. As a general guideline, at least one session should be spent on each goal or area of concern. For example, reasonable goals for a 6-week children-of-divorce group for second and third graders include gaining an accurate picture of the divorce process, normalizing the common experiences and feelings related to divorce, and providing a safe and supportive place to talk about divorce-related concerns. A self-esteem group for eighth graders might include the following goals: gaining an understanding of what self-esteem is and what role it plays in their lives, understanding how the attributions we make affect the way we view ourselves, identifying positive and negative attributions, learning how to dispute negative and irrational self-talk, and assessing actual skills in specific areas to gain a realistic sense of strengths and areas to improve.

As an example, to choose specific goals for children of divorce groups, DeLucia-Waack (2001) includes a checklist for potential group members of what situations are difficult for them. The situations correspond to specific group sessions. If a majority of the students indicate "I worry about what's going on with the lawyers or in court," then group sessions related to legal aspects of divorce will be included. The Morganett (1990) and Smead (1995) books both include pretests for different groups to help identify areas of concern.

Summary

Planning is essential to effective group work. The critical first step is to identify the potential group members and their needs in terms of skills and issues to be addressed. Based on this information, the type of group and goals for the group can be selected.

Learning Exercises

1. Interview a staff member in your setting about what the client needs are. What skills, interpersonal issues, and/or topics do clients need help with that could be impacted with a group intervention?

2. Select a journal relevant to the setting in which you are working. Peruse the contents for the past 2 years.

   a. Identify what group interventions have been suggested for this setting.

   b. Identify what interpersonal issues are discussed that also might be addressed with groups.

3

Rationale for Using Groups

Groups are not often seen as the preferred method of treatment for personal issues, as many misconceptions about group interventions exist, even though group counseling is an effective form of psychotherapy across different contexts and populations (Barlow, Burlingame, & Fuhriman, 2000; Burlingame, Fuhriman, & Mosier, 2003; Hoag & Burlingame, 1997; McDermut, Miller, & Brown, 2001; Payne & Marcus, 2008). Despite the comparable effectiveness of group, clients have historically preferred individual counseling, believing group to be less effective, attentive, and generally less appealing (Abraham, Lepisto, & Schultz, 1995; Subich & Coursol, 1985; Toseland & Siporin, 1986; Vogel, Shechtman, & Wade, 2010). In addition, despite knowledge to the contrary, therapists often share a negative bias toward group counseling (Piper, Ogrodniczuk, Joyce, & Weideman, 2011). This bias, expressed both in referrals from other counselors and in negative reactions from clients, will continue unless the misperceptions about groups and a clear rationale for why group intervention is the treatment of choice are carefully addressed and delineated. Group counseling expectations provide a specific context for studying the perceptions of individuals prior to engagement in group treatment. There is evidence that positive perceptions of groups are related to prior participation in individual or group counseling (Carter, Mitchell, & Krautheim, 2001; Slocum, 1987), as well as pro-group behaviors by the intake therapist (e.g., time spent talking about group as a treatment option; Carter et al., 2001). Nonetheless, group counseling expectations are more often not based on actual experiences or facts. The influence that counselors have over potential clients' choice of treatment options and the influence of academic and clinical training programs on their trainees make group counseling expectations an important construct to examine. This chapter helps group leaders develop a clear rationale for using a specific type of group and understanding why it will be helpful.

Why Group (and This Type of Group) to Address Group Goals?

A clear rationale for the use of a group intervention can include the potential benefits of using a group approach to achieve the stated goals, as well as empirical evidence supporting the use of group treatment for the specified problem. Group treatment has been shown to be as effective as individual treatment for a variety of problems (Burlingame, Fuhriman, & Johnson, 2002). More recently, Burlingame, Whitcomb, and Woodland (2013) emphasize that empirical evidence indicates that groups are the treatment of choice for a number of problems, such as anxiety, depression, and social skills. Specific chapters in the revised *Handbook of Group Counseling and Psychotherapy* (DeLucia-Waack, Kalodner, & Riva, 2013) suggest that there is much evidence and literature supporting and describing effective group interventions for specific settings, topics, and populations. For example, anger-management groups have been shown to be effective for children, adolescents, and adults (Fleckenstein & Horne, 2004). Villalba (2007) reported that psychoeducational groups in schools have demonstrated effectiveness in decreasing bullying behaviors, increasing self-esteem for children of alcoholics, decreasing trauma-related anxiety in young survivors of natural disasters, and decreasing anxiety and increasing academic performance for children of divorce. Studies of the effectiveness of many other types of groups can be found in the journals listed in Chapter 2. Burlingame et al. (2013) review more than 300 studies grouped by personal issue and systematically review support for group intervention.

This strong research support for the efficacy of groups clearly indicates that they are not simply watered-down individual treatment. While they have the advantage of being time- and cost-efficient, the group format provides a qualitatively different set of experiences that can be used to promote change. Many of the intrapersonal and interpersonal problems that bring both children and adults to counseling can be effectively addressed in the interpersonal setting of a group. The therapeutic factors inherent in groups, such as cohesion, universality, and interpersonal and vicarious learning, offer experiences and growth opportunities not readily available in individual treatment. These include, among others, a sense of belonging, awareness that one is not alone in one's struggles, the opportunity to give and receive feedback, and the chance to learn and practice new interpersonal skills.

Group members respond well to groups as a place to openly share their personal concerns and problems. The relational nature of groups can be beneficial for children dealing with stressors or problems that result in feelings of rejection, anger, alienation, and isolation. Groups also provide group members, specifically children and adolescents, an opportunity to learn and practice new skills in a safe and supportive peer environment.

A counseling group for those who have been victims of abuse, for example, provides a safe environment to rebuild trust in relationships. In a group setting, participants can express their full range of mixed emotions related to their perpetrators, regain a sense of control and mastery, and establish a positive self-image. At the same time, addressing these goals in a group setting allows group members to establish relationships with others who have had similar experiences (Corey, Corey, & Corey, 2010), emphasizing universality and normalizing their experiences.

Groups are an excellent fit with the developmental transitions of adolescence. The important role of peer relationships and the interpersonal nature of many of their struggles make the group format particularly appropriate for this age group. By harnessing the power of peer influence, groups offer several developmentally valuable experiences, including the opportunity to practice new skills and behaviors, to give and receive support, to learn from the differing ideas and opinions of others, to learn about oneself through feedback from others, and to improve reasoning skills through discussions with peers (Akos, Hamm, Mack, & Dunaway, 2007).

A psychoeducational conflict-management group for adolescents in schools is an opportunity for students to learn appropriate interpersonal behaviors for the expression of anger. In addition to skills training and behavioral rehearsal, the group format allows adolescents to share their own experiences and concerns and engage in mutual problem solving. Developmentally, this exchange of thoughts and feelings with peers is an important experience that promotes increased interpersonal awareness, perspective taking, and reasoning (Fleckenstein & Horne, 2004).

Whether feelings of isolation and depression; relational conflicts with spouses, friends, or coworkers; or lingering maladaptive patterns that result from childhood experiences, interpersonal difficulties are at the heart of many problems faced by adults as well (Chen & Rybak, 2004). As such, the group format can be an excellent means of helping adults learn about their relational needs and patterns. As described by Shulman (2011), in groups members can

> make the connection to the relationship problems that initially brought them to the group. In effect, the group member acts out the problem in the group almost as if to say "Do you want to see how I get messed up in my relationships? Watch!" (p. 525)

Adults can gain insight about the nature of their interpersonal difficulties, gain support from others experiencing similar concerns, and practice skills for relating with others more effectively outside the group.

Groups for adults can be organized by topic or can be general interpersonal groups in which members' presenting problems are heterogeneous in nature. Topic-oriented groups can be powerful catalysts when organized around common developmental needs or concerns of members (Corey et al., 2010). More general interpersonal growth groups have the advantage of members working on different issues, allowing for increased interpersonal learning, vicarious learning, and feedback exchange.

How Does the Conceptual Framework Used Explain How Goals Will Be Achieved?

Designing an effective group requires an underlying theory to serve as a road map. When combined with the purpose of the group and leader techniques to be used, this creates a coherent framework to guide the group leader in the many planning and intervention decisions he or she must make. The Association for Specialists in Group Work *Best Practice Guidelines* (Thomas & Pender, 2008) state that "Group Workers develop and are able to articulate a general conceptual framework to guide practice and a rationale for use of techniques" (p. 2).

Day (2013) describes interpersonal learning theory as a conceptual framework that underlies most types of groups. Interpersonal learning theory posits that through the activation of self-schemas, group members interact in the social climate of the group in ways that are similar to how they interact in other relationships in their lives. In other words, as described by Arokwitz (1992), "our past experiences skew our present environment and often lead us to create the very conditions that perpetuate our problems in a kind of vicious circle" (p. 269). The change process in groups involves members having new learning experiences that disconfirm their original faulty schemas. These new experiences allow individuals to become more flexible in their interpersonal interactions.

From within this general framework, different types of groups may emphasize different aspects of cognitive, affective, and/or behavioral change, with different sets of goals and identified techniques for achieving them. They may also incorporate additional theoretical concepts, such as an explicit cognitive-behavioral emphasis on maladaptive thought and behavior patterns. This type of group might include teaching techniques such as goal setting, planning, modeling, and monitoring of identified behaviors. Many resources are available that provide applications of various theoretical models and types of groups to specific populations. What is essential is that group leaders have a coherent view of the conceptual framework from which they will be working, and how that links to the group's goals, individual members' goals, and the content and process components and techniques they will use. This framework will provide clarity and direction to the leader and members, and also will allow the leader to provide a clear rationale to gain external support for the group, which is discussed below.

Agency and School Support

Formal and informal support is essential throughout the school or agency in which groups are being led. Administrative support is needed so that resources are allotted (time, money, space, personnel) and appropriate procedures are followed. In addition, colleagues must understand and support the use of groups to refer group members appropriately. However, the misunderstandings and potential biases against groups that may exist for both counselors and potential group members may also extend to administrators and other important individuals within the agency or school setting where a group program may be beneficial. If these individuals do not see how groups can support the mission of the organization, or believe that groups are unnecessary or second-rate treatment, they are unlikely to make referrals or lend the support necessary to ensure the success of a group program.

On a broad level, Whittingham (2013) suggested that group leaders work to transform an organizational climate in which the use of groups is questioned to one in which the question is, "Why *not* group?" To accomplish this shift, group leaders not only must understand and be able to articulate the value of groups, but they must also be able to offer a rationale that links the use of groups to the mission and goals of the organization. For example, in a correctional setting, a counseling group may be targeted toward improving interpersonal relationships to support reintegration of inmates with their families, thereby reducing the likelihood of recidivism. In a high school, the use of peer mentoring groups for freshmen can be targeted toward increasing students' sense of connectedness to school, which has been demonstrated to aid in reducing both dropout and behavior problems (Manning, 2005). In both examples, the benefits can be clearly delineated for the individual members and the organization as a whole.

To further support an organizational shift to "Why *not* group?" administrators and colleagues need to have a solid grasp of the group modality and the role they can play in supporting groups. Administrators may not have an understanding of groups beyond large-group instruction, or may view all groups as intense therapy groups that are not appropriate for their particular setting. Teachers may view groups as yet another distraction from instructional time and not see how the goals of the group can support student success in their classrooms. Even other counseling colleagues may have had insufficient group training and prefer to default to individual counseling approaches with which they are more comfortable (Whittingham, 2013). Group leaders can gain support from administrators and colleagues through orientations or in-house trainings that explore the research on group efficacy as related to their organizational mission, as well as by providing them clear information and instructions about referral and screening procedures (Whittingham, 2013).

Understanding and addressing the specific concerns and potential barriers to success in any organization and the key individuals within that organization will allow leaders to address these concerns more effectively. Administrators, teachers, and counseling professionals may have different concerns and need different information to fully support a group program; these concerns are addressed below.

Administration

Leaders of a group must decide what channels to take to obtain approval for leading this group in their school or agency. Does a proposal need to be submitted? To whom should the proposal be submitted? What should the proposal include? In general, a thorough proposal should include (a) a rationale for the group based on current counseling literature and research, along with a needs assessment of the population to be served; (b) goals, format, and duration of the group; (c) recruitment, screening, selection, and consent procedures; (d) specific interventions and activities; and (e) evaluation procedures. In a school setting, permission may be needed from any or all of the following people: the head of counseling or guidance services, the principal, the director of pupil services, the superintendent, and/or the school board. In an agency, permission may be needed from the director of clinical services, the director of the agency, and/or the board of directors. When proposing a psychoeducational group, it is important to clarify the purpose, goals, and population to be served. The common misperception that all groups are group therapy and, thus, all long-term and directed at persons with severe problems often needs to be disputed.

Coworkers

Coworkers also need to understand the goals, targeted population, and typical interventions to be used in a group. In agencies, counseling practitioners need to believe in the efficacy of groups to convey with a sense of enthusiasm information about how groups work for potential members, because how groups as a treatment modality are presented to potential members can greatly influence their willingness to participate. In addition, counselors need to understand the specific inclusion and exclusion criteria for a given group to make appropriate referrals.

Similarly, in a school setting, teachers need to believe in the efficacy of groups if they are to allow students to be taken out of their classrooms. As noted above, it is especially important to help teachers understand how participating in a group will help the student function better in the classroom both academically and socially. The dilemma for teachers is often that with increasing academic standards, those students who struggle the most personally also struggle academically, and missing class time means falling even farther behind. Group leaders need to help teachers understand the value of groups and also to work with the teachers to maximize the value of participating in a group while minimizing the possible impact of missed class time. Such techniques as rotating the time of the group each week so that students will miss a class only once every 7 or 8 weeks, notifying a teacher ahead of time so that missed work may be done in advance or at home, and allowing students to come late to group after taking a quiz are all helpful.

As suggested earlier, the more information provided to teachers about what happens in psychoeducational groups, the better. Regardless of the theme of a psychoeducational group, the focus is on teaching social skills that are relevant to classroom behavior. If teachers can reinforce these newly learned behaviors for group members (and other students in the classroom), the whole school community benefits. Teachers are not trained extensively in psychosocial and developmental issues of children, and the more information counseling professionals can provide about these issues, the more teachers will understand and be helpful to children. Group work specialists who provide Changing Family Groups throughout Central Ohio suggested that "acquainting teachers with the effects of family transition on children, information about the group, and the benefits children receive by participating, are important" (Beech Acres Airing Institute, 1993, p. 9).

Summary

A clear rationale for the use of a group intervention is important to guide the planning of your group. This rationale should include a conceptual framework for achieving your intended group goals, a grasp of the research literature supporting the efficacy of group interventions to meet your intended goals, and considerations of both the developmental needs of your target population and the mission of your organization. Developing this type of rationale will not only provide you with a road map for implementing your group but also serve as a means of gaining support from administrators, colleagues, and potential group members.

Learning Exercises

1. Develop a proposal for a specific group you would like to conduct in your current or intended work setting. Target the proposal to a specific person, such as the school principal. Include the need and rationale for the group, explain how the group methodology is important to address the need, and highlight how the group will support the mission of the organization.

2. Write a paragraph that you might use to discuss the value of joining a group in your current or intended work setting, compared with other types of treatment options, to a potential group member. Consider what specific hesitations or concerns the potential member might have and how you could most effectively respond to them.

4 Making Decisions About Your Group Based on Best Practices in Group Work

The structure and length of groups is very different depending on the type of group, the issues to be addressed, and/or the population. Groups for children and adolescents are different from those for adults. In addition, psychoeducational groups tend to be briefer in terms of number of sessions and session length but more structured, with activities designed to facilitate discussion of a topic and/or development of new skills and behaviors, than are counseling groups. The Association for Specialists in Group Work *Best Practice Guidelines* (Thomas & Pender, 2008) includes a section on planning that focuses on pregroup decision making. This chapter addresses these planning areas, with specific suggestions about group size, composition, number of sessions, and session length.

Gender Mix and Group Size and Composition

Based on the goals of the group, a decision must be made as to how many group members to include and the composition likely to work best for this particular group. Ideal group size varies according to the age of the children, beginning with a group size of three to six for younger children, five to seven for children ages 6 to 9, and up to eight for preteen and teen groups. Psychoeducational groups may include up to 12 adults, while counseling groups function best with six to eight group members. Projected attendance may also be a factor in how many are invited to participate in a group. If there is a high rate of absenteeism, it may be useful to include one or two more group members so that there is always a critical mass for each group session. For therapeutic factors to work, there needs to be enough group members for interaction to occur. It is very hard to lead a group consisting of two coleaders and two group members, even with group members who require a lot of attention. The interaction is limited, and it is hard to get members to interact with each other rather than with the leaders.

There are several important considerations regarding group composition. Depending on its purpose and goals, a group may function best when its membership is homogeneous or heterogeneous. Psychoeducational groups generally benefit from a membership that is homogeneous regarding the topic to be addressed in the group but heterogeneous in terms of individual members' needs and goals related to the topic. For example, in an anger-management group, all members should clearly be experiencing some difficulties with their anger. However, the group is likely to be most effective if members have different styles of dealing with their anger and/or different individual goals related to anger management. This composition allows for enhanced interpersonal learning to take place, as members are able to explore their own experiences in relation to those of others.

In counseling and therapy groups, which are more broadly focused on interpersonal growth and in which the group process is the primary mechanism of change, a heterogeneous membership is likely to be more effective. This creates a social microcosm in which, as described by Corey, Corey, and Corey (2010), "members can experiment with new behavior and develop interpersonal skills with the help of feedback from a rich variety of people in an environment that represents everyday reality" (p. 118).

Another important group composition consideration is gender. It is ultimately up to the style and experience of the group leader whether to lead mixed- or single-gender groups. Some counselors report that the diversity in emotions and reactions in mixed groups enhances effectiveness (Kalter, 1998). Some suggest single-gender groups in middle school to lessen the self-consciousness and reluctance to self-disclose that may result from boys and girls being in the same group (Hines & Fields, 2002). Carrell (2000) suggested using mixed-gender groups for older teens because so much of their focus and concern is on relationships.

Issues of cultural diversity in group membership must also be considered during the planning of a group. A lack of attention to culture on the part of the group leader can result in premature dropout by group members or unspoken difficulties that impede the group's progress toward its stated goals. Merchant (2009) identified three types of diversity-related groups. *Culture-specific groups* focus on a specific cultural population or the needs of individuals who share common experiences related to diversity. In this type of group, members should be of the same or similar cultural backgrounds so that "the shared cultural context allows a safe space for group members to engage in self exploration and problem resolution, without added pressure to explain or teach others about their culture" (p. 14). *Interpersonal learning groups* are designed for the purpose of promoting greater understanding across cultural groups. Such groups will include an intentional mix of members from different cultural backgrounds that are the focus of the group. *Other-content–focused groups* are those that have a primary focus on some other topic (i.e., substance abuse or domestic violence) but pay careful attention to the diversity among members as an important group issue. This is the type of group most frequently discussed in this book. That is, while the group's primary focus is on either a psychoeducational topic or on general counseling or therapy goals, attention to diversity is important throughout the planning process.

In terms of diversity of group composition, Merchant (2009) offers several important considerations. Will a group member feel like the "only one" different from the rest of the group, or will members feel supported for their diversity? Should the group membership be expanded or altered to allow for greater diversity to support a member who is from a minority group? Using an inclusive definition of diversity that encompasses not only race and ethnicity but also culture, religious and spiritual beliefs, sexual orientation, socioeconomic status, and abilities (Rapin & Keel, 1998), leaders should be purposeful in considering membership diversity and its impact on the group as a whole. The newly revised Association for Specialists in Group Work *Multicultural and Social Justice Competence Principles for Group Workers* (Singh, Merchant, Skudrzyk, & Ingene, 2012) provides specific guidelines for attention to diversity in all aspects of group work.

Length and Number of Sessions

The ideal length of the group sessions also varies according to the age of the group members: 20 to 30 minutes is optimal with children aged 6 and under, 30 to 40 minutes with children aged 6 to 9, and 40 to 75 minutes with those older than 9 (Gazda, 1989; Thompson & Rudolph, 1988). A session length between 1 and 1 ½ hours is typical for psychoeducational and counseling groups for adults.

The duration of the group, or number of sessions, will vary by the type of group as well as by the setting. An ideal length for most psychoeducational groups in this setting is 12 to 16 sessions, allowing time to deal with more complex issues and for behavior change to occur (the old adage is that it takes 10 weeks to acquire a new habit or behavior). Counseling and therapy groups will typically be of a longer duration—anywhere from 10 to 15 weeks to a year or more.

The duration of a group will also be impacted by the setting in which the group occurs. Mental health agencies, for example, may be able to sustain longer groups. Court-referred groups, on the other hand, may significantly vary with regard to length. For children and adolescents who are attending court-referred groups due to a parental problem or issue, the group will most likely be short-term and prevention focused—that is, one 4- or 8-hour session or four 2-hour sessions focused on how to adjust to parents divorcing. For students who are court referred for their own actions (i.e., fighting, drug use), the number of sessions is generally longer. Even though the population is at risk, these groups are also typically structured and focused on skill development, such as anger-management skills, stress management, problem-solving skills, life skills, and cognitive restructuring or criminal thinking errors (Morgan, 2004).

Regardless of the duration of the group, the first session or two must be devoted to the establishment of ground rules and goals for the group, the introduction of members, and development. At the end of the group, at least one session, if not two, must be devoted to termination, with the goals of helping members summarize what they have learned, express their feelings about the group and group members, and discuss how they will use what they have learned outside of group. Thus, a general guideline to determine how many sessions are needed would be to include one to two sessions for introduction, one to two sessions for termination, and one to two sessions for each goal scheduled to be addressed.

Summary

Pregroup decision making is essential to successful groups. The size of the group (number of members), number of sessions, length of sessions, and gender composition of the group depend on the goals of the group, type of group, and potential group members.

Learning Exercises

1. Find an article in a recent journal (2005 or later) that describes a group intervention for a specific population. What is recommended for

   - group size,
   - group composition, and
   - number of sessions and session length?

2. Identify an example of each type of group described by Merchant (2009). Merchant identified three types of diversity-related groups:

   - *Culture-specific groups*
   - *Interpersonal learning groups*
   - *Other-content–focused groups*

   Compare and contrast these groups based on

   - group size,
   - group composition, and
   - number of sessions and session length.

5 Group Leader Preparation

Group leadership has been shown to influence group cohesion, impact, and effectiveness.

Successful groups, characterized by accomplishment and personal satisfaction, are those in which people

- feel listened to;
- are accepted for their individuality;
- have a voice;
- are part of a climate in which leaders and members acknowledge and appreciate varied perspectives, needs, and concerns;
- understand and support the purpose of the group; and
- have the opportunity to contribute to the accomplishment of particular tasks. (Hulse-Killacky, Killacky, & Donigian, 2001, p. 6)

Because of the complexity of group work in comparison with individual counseling, it is imperative for group leaders to carefully plan and prepare for each group they lead. This chapter highlights important areas to address as group leaders begin to prepare for a group experience.

Guidelines for Practice

The Association for Specialists in Group Work (ASGW) published the *Professional Standards for the Training of Group Workers* (Wilson, Rapin, & Haley-Banez, 2000) with two goals: (1) to identify four types of groups (i.e., task/work, psychoeducational/guidance, counseling, and psychotherapy groups) and (2) to specify the focus and goals of each group and training activities for each type of group. These standards are unique in that they clearly define the four types of group work, their focus, group leadership skills and knowledge needed, and specific training experiences. In addition, the more recently revised ASGW *Best Practice Guidelines* (Thomas & Pender, 2008) suggest that "Group Workers choose techniques and a leadership style appropriate to the type(s) of group(s) being offered" (p. 113) and "Group Workers apply and modify knowledge, skills and techniques" (p. 115). Group leadership skills must be tailored to the group type and stage, and to the unique needs of various cultural and ethnic groups. The newly revised ASGW *Multicultural and Social Justice Competence Principles for Group Workers* (Singh, Merchant, Skudrzyk, & Ingene, 2012) emphasizes the importance of recognizing diversity in group members and specifically suggests that group leaders "seek to understand the extent to which general group leadership skills and functions may be appropriate or inappropriate for group work facilitation with multicultural group members" (p. 4) and "model relationship skills essential for connecting with and creating connections between multicultural group members while planning, performing, and processing groups" (p. 5).

In addition, the American Group Psychotherapy Association (2007) *Practice Guidelines for Group Psychotherapy* assert that "many of the principles articulated here are relevant to diverse group therapy approaches which employ a variety of techniques, with various client populations, and in a variety of treatment or service settings" (p. 3). Salazar (2009) is an excellent resource for selecting and processing activities around diversity and multicultural counseling in groups. The Bauman and Steen (2010, 2012) DVDs on multicultural groups for children and adolescents illustrate effective group leadership when working with a diverse group.

Leadership Skills and Interventions

Effective leadership is an essential component of any group; the skills and behaviors of the leader impact both the process of the group and its outcomes (Riva, Wachtel, & Lasky, 2004). The skills necessary for successful group leadership include, but are not limited to, those necessary for effective individual counseling. As described by Luke (2013), "group skills are distinguished from individual counseling skills and other prescribed interventions because they stimulate interaction within and between group members, in addition to promoting therapeutic factors and whole group development" (p. 3). Group leader interventions can range from the implementation of planned and structured activities to interventions that are utilized in response to specific incidents or member behaviors as they occur. Additionally, interventions can be directed toward individuals, subgroups of members, or to the group as a whole. The range of skills and interventions that are potentially useful in groups is wide. "Almost any intervention can be appropriate at almost any group stage, provided that it is appropriately geared to the readiness of members and the issues being dealt with at that point in the group" (Morran, Stockton, & Whittingham, 2004, p. 93).

One framework for classifying interventions is that originally identified by Lieberman, Yalom, and Miles (1973), which included four categories of effective group leadership behaviors: caring, emotional stimulation, meaning attribution, and executive skills. Luke (2013) identified as essential nine behaviors that fit within these categories. Luke emphasized that effective leadership skills will vary by group stage, type of group, and group goals.

Caring

Caring interventions include those that help group members feel safe, cared about, and accepted so that they can make the most of their group experience by participating, helping others, taking risks, giving feedback, and trying out new behaviors. The goal is to help members feel that they are a valued part of the group and that sharing of their experiences and perceptions is valued. Morran et al. (2004) suggested that active listening skills are an essential part of creating this culture of caring. Early in a group, this may involve directly reassuring members and encouraging or reinforcing their active participation or efforts to take risks in sharing or self-disclosing. Skills in this category may be similar to those in individual counseling, including offering warmth, empathy, support, positive regard, acceptance, genuineness, and concern. Additionally, active listening, reflecting thoughts and feelings, summarizing, and clarifying are important leadership skills in this category.

Empirical support for these interventions includes results of a review of 135 studies that found that group members benefited from positive leader behavior such as warmth, support, and genuine interest (Dies, 1994). Similarly, Yalom (1995) identified a positive linear relationship between caring and positive group outcomes; that is, the higher the caring, the higher the positive outcome.

It is important to note that the importance of high levels of caring does not mean that members should never be challenged. Corey and Corey (2010) cautioned against premature or excessive supporting interventions that foster dependency or prevent members from experiencing their own conflicts and dealing with them independently. Similarly, a common misconception about groups is that if people care, they will not say anything that could hurt someone's feelings or make them feel uncomfortable. The dilemma inherent in this misperception is that sometimes people have "blind spots" or do not know when they have made a mistake or done something that negatively impacts others. Group feedback is vital to learning new ways of interacting; giving and receiving constructive feedback is an important aspect of all groups.

Emotional Stimulation

Emotional stimulation interventions are those that help group members make a personal connection to what is happening in the group, identify and explore feelings, and connect feelings to behaviors. Morran et al. (2004) described these interventions as those intended to energize and engage members in the work of the group.

There is a large number of potential interventions in this category. *Drawing out* involves directly inviting members to participate or become involved in a particular discussion or activity. *Modeling* occurs when leaders demonstrate desired group member behaviors, such as interpersonal communication, the exchange of feedback, sharing of here-and-now experiences, and appropriate self-disclosure. *Linking* is used to connect the thoughts, feelings, or experiences of members to each other. Doing so promotes member interaction and engagement and builds cohesion, trust, and universality.

Leader *self-disclosure* involves group leaders sharing their own experiences or here-and-now reactions in the group. When leaders share their here-and-now reactions in the group process, it can be used to model this type of sharing for members, as well as to enhance or deepen the group process. Guidelines for using self-disclosure include (1) when the information or reaction is directly related to what is happening in the group, (2) when it models a desired behavior for group members, or (3) where a direct benefit to the group is anticipated (Morran et al., 2004).

Leaders can *encourage feedback* to allow members to better understand themselves and what is necessary for personal growth and behavior change. This involves both members and leaders sharing their personal reactions and insights about each other and critical events in the group. To promote the effective exchange of feedback, positive feedback should be emphasized during initial group sessions; in later stages, a balance of positive and corrective feedback should be included. Feedback is most effective when it is specific and behavioral (rather than global and emotional; Morran, Stockton, & Harris, 1991). Negative or corrective feedback is also most effective when it is followed by, or sandwiched between, positive feedback (Morran, Stockton, Cline, & Teed, 1998).

Yalom (1995) reported a curvilinear relationship between emotional stimulation and group outcomes; that is, too much or too little of this type of behavior resulted in less positive outcomes. There is also support for the efficacy of the specific interventions in this category. For example, feedback has been linked to increased motivation for change and greater insight into how one's behavior affects others, as well as members' rating their experience more positively. Modeling has been shown to be effective in increasing desired member behaviors. Dies (1994) found that behaviors displayed by the leader, including feedback delivery and acceptance and here-and-now communications, led to increases in those same behaviors by group members. Linking has also received much support in the group literature (Morran et al., 2004).

Meaning Attribution

Interventions to promote meaning attribution are those intended to help members make meaning of what happens during the group experience, learn from it, and apply this learning to their lives. To accomplish this, the emphasis of these interventions is on explanation, clarification, interpretation, and provision of concepts to help members understand their thoughts, feelings, and behaviors. Yalom (1995) reported a positive linear relationship between meaning attribution and group outcome; the higher the meaning attribution, the higher the positive outcomes.

An important skill in this category is *interpretation,* or offering possible explanations for events, behaviors, thoughts, and feelings to promote insight. Interpretations help provide a cognitive framework for making meaning of the many experiences and interactions that occur within a group. Research suggests that leader interpretations help members integrate complex personal and group-related events, thus encouraging their investment in the group experience, and facilitate generalizations for group experiences to personal experiences outside of the group. Interpretations about the client's impact on the environment and his or her patterns of behavior were most associated with client change.

Processing is essential for promoting meaning attribution. The experience of a group event or activity is rarely growth producing; rather, the meaning that members draw from it is what leads to growth. Processing involves

> capitalizing on significant happenings in the here-and-now interactions of the group to help members reflect on the meaning of their experience, better understand their own thoughts and feelings and actions, and generalize what is learned to their life outside of the group. (Stockton, Morran, & Nitza, 2000, p. 345)

The ability to process group events is a key component of effective group leadership. One of the most common mistakes novice group leaders make is not processing activities or events. Expert leaders, however, emphasize the use of processing to maximize exploration, learning, and change in groups (Rubel & Kline, 2008). As described by Ward (2013),

> Effective leaders must identify significant individual, interpersonal, and group events, understand and develop hypotheses about the meaning of these critical incidents, and then use this knowledge in order to select and organize microskills and more complex interventions in order to help members to identify, explore, discover, and apply new meanings in their in-group and out-of-group interactions. (p. 9)

Ward (2013) provides an overview of existing models of group processing to guide group leaders and suggests the use of journaling and supervision to enhance processing skills. Bridbord (2006) provides suggestions for processing activities in all group stages, while Bridbord and Nitza (2008) specifically address processing activities in groups in the schools. Jacobs and Schimmel (2009) provide guidelines for effective processing activities related to multicultural counseling and diversity. Further information about processing is provided in Book 6 in this kit.

Executive Functions

Executive functions are those skills used to create structure and promote safety so that members can participate effectively in the group. In other words, they are intended to provide a group climate conducive to trust, openness, and cohesion. Structure plays an important role in group development (Dies, 1994). Generally, group leaders should provide more structure in the initial sessions to establish group norms, clarify group and individual goals, and provide sufficient safety to encourage members to begin the process of self-disclosure and self-exploration. During middle sessions, structure can gradually be reduced as members learn how the group works and begin to take more responsibility for its functioning. However, increased structure is needed again during the final sessions to ensure that group members have gained insight into what they have learned, how they have learned it, and how they will apply what they have learned to their lives.

Providing appropriate structure can begin with the *establishment of group norms and ground rules*. It is important to frame the creation of ground rules as necessary for members to feel safe, try out new behaviors, and give feedback within the group. Such questions as, "What do we need to do to keep this group safe?" and "What do we need to do as members to help each other learn new behaviors?" can be helpful in beginning this discussion.

Other skills in this category include those that protect members from undue pressure, confrontation or attacks, or inappropriate self-disclosure. *Blocking* is a specific type of protection used to stop a member from acting inappropriately. Blocking can be used to stop a member who is self-disclosing too much too soon, or at a level that is significantly more intimate than the level of the other members. It can also be used to stop excessive storytelling or rambling, or to intervene to prevent excessive probing, gossiping, or invading the privacy of others. Research suggests that group members frequently attribute damaging experiences to undue confrontation, criticism, and pressure to self-disclose by other members. Blocking is an essential intervention that can be used to prevent such experiences and can often be followed by other types of interventions that allow members to interact in a more helpful way.

Focusing interventions are executive functions that direct or redirect the group to a different topic or activity for that particular group session. Focusing interventions are often used as part of the opening of the group to introduce the topic for that session. Group leaders often also gently remind group members of the task or topic at hand when they begin to go off on tangents or provide details that are not relevant to the current activity. Focusing interventions are also used as part of the processing of the group as a reminder of what has happened in group that session, and as a lead-in to asking group members what they have learned and how they will apply it.

An additional framework for conceptualizing group leadership skills is that of the levels of the group system to be targeted. As described previously, interventions can be targeted at the intrapersonal, interpersonal, and/or group-as-a-whole levels. Luke (2013) provided a useful organization of nine leadership skills within these three levels. In her framework, intrapersonal skills are those that focus on the internal thoughts, feelings, and experiences of individual group members, and they include *support*, *drawing out*, and *blocking*. Luke noted that these interventions may be overused in groups and suggested that these intrapersonal interventions are likely most useful in the initial phases of a group. Interventions at the interpersonal level, as described by Luke, are those that focus on "group members' relationships, interactions, and communications both with one another and the group leader" (p. 12). She argues that these are essential but perhaps underutilized interventions and includes *modeling, linking*, and *feedback* in this category. Finally, group-as-a-whole interventions are those that involve norm setting, group development, and overall group dynamics, and they include *reframing, self-disclosure*, and *processing*. Luke notes that these can be powerful interventions in promoting group learning if they are not overused.

It is important to emphasize that many of the interventions described here overlap, and many other interventions may also be useful. Leaders should select interventions based on the type of group, the stage of group development, and the needs of specific group members. Overall, as described in a recent review of effective group leadership, "leaders will want to be positive, supportive, provide sufficient structure, attend to developing group cohesion, allow group members to take ownership of their group, and provide a meaningful context for what occurs in the group" (Riva et al., 2004, p. 45).

Coleadership

Coleadership for groups is preferable for efficiency and theoretical reasons, sometimes specifically a male–female coleadership team. The benefits of coleadership are helpful in any group: two role models, two leaders who cooperate and work together, and two sets of eyes and ears to observe the content and process of the group. It is suggested that coleadership is better for a variety of reasons, such as efficiency (e.g., the group can still continue if one leader is sick or unavailable), effectiveness (e.g., two leaders can track group members more easily), supervision and training of new group therapists, or as a way to model healthy communication patterns (e.g., male/female interactions) between coleaders in front of the group members (Dies, 1994; Shapiro, 1999). It is also theorized that coleaders who model appropriate interaction between themselves, such as in resolving disagreements or compromising, will have group members who demonstrate better skills in these areas as well. In addition, a male–female coleadership team can model collaboration between male and female adults, and provide contact with supportive and caring adults of both sexes. While such a model of coleadership may be time intensive and difficult to arrange, it is highly valuable and worth the effort.

Regardless of their skills and experience, coleaders must commit to weekly planning and supervision sessions to prepare for their group and to process what has happened. A dedicated hour each week is essential to working cooperatively with a coleader. The time is spent planning individual goals and strategies for each group member, reviewing session events and group process, and planning for future sessions. When coleadership is not possible, a group leader leading a group by him- or herself should still set aside an hour a week to plan and process for the group.

To prepare for the group, leaders need to think about it from several different perspectives. How will they as counselors prepare for the group personally and professionally? How will they prepare others for the group—specifically, their school or agency (including administrators), parents, and group members? What are their beliefs about the nature of the problem, the symptoms, possible causes, and interventions, and how best a group can help these group members? To do this, personal values and experiences with the particular problem area must be explored. To begin to establish trust and cooperation, coleaders should meet regularly before the group starts to discuss theoretical orientation, leadership style, and goals and interventions for the group. Each coleader should assess his or her strengths and weaknesses as a leader of the particular group being planned. Assessment of the group leadership skills needed for this group should include the type of group (psychoeducational or counseling), the age of group members, and the focus and goals of the group. The *Co-Facilitator Inventory* (Pfeiffer & Jones, 1970) and *Group Leadership Questionnaire* (Wile, Bron, & Pollack, 1970) provide specific situations that may occur in group as a stimulus for discussion. Also available are several self-assessment instruments related to group leadership style and behaviors that can be completed individually and then discussed between coleaders. *Critical Incidents in Group Counseling* (Tyson, Perusse, & Whitledge, 2004) also provides specific incidents, with group leaders' suggestions on how to work with them as they occur in groups.

While previous models of group leadership development vary in the number and emphasis of stages, Dugo and Beck (1997), drawing from earlier models in the literature, suggested a coleadership model of development that consisted of nine phases: Phase 1, "Creating a Contract"; Phase 2, "Forming an Identity"; Phase 3, "Building a Cooperative Team"; Phase 4, "Developing Closeness"; Phase 5, "Defining Strengths and Limitations"; Phase 6, "Exploring Possibilities"; Phase 7, "Supporting Self-Confrontation"; Phase 8, "Integrating and Implementing Changes"; and Phase 9, "Closing." Dugo and Beck emphasize Phase 1 as essential to becoming an effective cotherapy team and insist that cotherapists should not lead a group together unless they have at least reached Phase 3. Bridbord and DeLucia-Waack (2011), based on a study of 54 coleadership pairs, concluded that coleaders' perceived theoretical compatibility and differences in coleader confrontation leadership style best predicted coleadership relationship satisfaction, emphasizing the importance of coleaders' working together to develop a joint leadership style.

Training of Multicultural-Competent Group Leaders

The ASGW *Multicultural and Social Justice Competence Principles for Group Workers* (Singh et al., 2012) specifies three competencies: awareness of self, awareness of group members' worldview, and diversity-appropriate intervention strategies. DeLucia-Waack and Donigian's (2004) model expands on these principles with four steps:

Step 1: Examine your own culture, ethnic values, and racial identity to understand who you are as a person.

Step 2: Examine your beliefs about group work and the inherent assumptions within the Eurocentric view of group work.

Step 3: Learn about other cultures in terms of what they value and how these values may affect group work.

Step 4: Develop your personal plan for group work that emphasizes and utilizes cultural diversity guidelines for leading effective multicultural groups.

Resource Gathering

There are different categories of essential resources needed when planning for a group. They include general resources related to best practices in group work, information for how to lead psychoeducational groups, and also references specific to the type of group to be led. Journals focused on group work, such as *Journal for Specialists in Group Work, Small Group, Small Group Research, Group, Group Dynamics, International Journal of Group Work,* and *Social Work in Groups,* all include the latest theory, practice, and research related to groups. Websites for professional group organizations also provide resource sections that can be helpful, such as those for ASGW (hwww.asgw.org), American Group Psychotherapy Association (www.agpa.org), Society of Group Psychology and Group Psychotherapy (www.apadivisions.org/division-49/index.aspx), and International Association for Social Work with Groups (http://iaswg.org).

Supervision

Supervision and/or consultation with other group workers is an integral part of effective and ethical group work. Yalom (1995) found that without supervision, group therapists were not able to identify mistakes and generate new plans of action; instead, they became stuck in a cycle of repeated ineffective interventions. Group leadership is a complex process different from other forms of counseling. As described by Riva (2013), group leadership requires a multidimensional focus in which leaders must respond to "limitless situations that are beyond the scope of individual therapy" (p. 11). In addition to individual members' growth and progress toward goals, group leaders must attend to member-to-member and member-to-leader interactions, as well as group-as-a-whole dynamics, among many other considerations. Thus, supervision is important even for experienced individual therapists as they develop into skilled group leaders (Riva, 2013).

Several models of supervision of group leadership are possible. Supervision may consist of one group leader consulting with a supervisor about his or her work, dyadic supervision in which a more experienced group leader coleads with a less experienced trainee, triadic supervision in which both members of a coleadership team meet with a supervisor, or group supervision of group leaders (DeLucia-Waack & Fauth, 2004). Regardless of the model chosen, supervision should include "assessing progress on group and member goals, leader behaviors and techniques, group dynamics and interventions, developing understanding, and acceptance of meaning" (Rapin & Keel, 1998, p. 243). The type of group being led should also inform the emphasis of the supervision. For example, topics and skills to be addressed in supervision of a psychoeducational group might include effective management of time, providing structure to the sessions and redirecting the focus as necessary, and assisting members in setting and working on concrete goals (Riva, 2013). For counseling and psychotherapy groups, supervision may emphasize using group dynamics as learning opportunities, identifying and working with group events that relate to members' concerns and goals, and dealing effectively with interpersonal conflict in the group (Riva, 2013).

It is useful to think of the focus of supervision as having three parts—conceptualizing the case, planning and evaluating the effectiveness of techniques and interventions, and exploring personal reactions to group events and members—with the goal of each being effective group leadership behavior. Case conceptualization for group work includes a theoretical perspective both of the group as a whole, in terms of group stages, and of specific members, in terms of personal growth and development. Where is the group in its development? Are individual members making progress toward their goals? What is happening in group that facilitates progress toward individual member goals? What is happening in group that hinders progress toward individual member goals?

With a clear conceptualization of the group dynamics and process, supervision can address identification of interventions, techniques, and leader behaviors appropriate for the specific needs of the group, as well as the evaluation of those from previous sessions. An emphasis on skill development is also important and can include role play and other opportunities for group leaders to gain confidence in their abilities (Riva, 2013). Discussion of personal reactions to clients and group incidents is also helpful in understanding how clients and group events affect the other members, the group as a whole, each coleader, the coleader relationship, and the supervisory relationships. Personal reactions to clients often may interfere with the planning and execution of specific interventions. At other times, personal reactions to a group member or an incident in a group session may be similar to what others in group experienced, thus providing important information about what is happening in group. Issues of leader anxiety, parallel process, countertransference, and the coleader relationship are also important potential topics for exploration (Corey & Corey, 2010; Gladding, 2003).

DeLucia-Waack (2002) suggested a format for each supervision session that allows time for discussion, planning, and processing. It includes the following steps:

Reporting of what specifically happened in the most recent group session in terms of events, member behavior, and leader behavior and reactions. What happened? Who sat where? Who did what? Who said what? How did members react, verbally and nonverbally?

Reflection on what happened in the most recent group session. What worked? What didn't work? What felt productive? When did it feel as though the group was working or making progress? When didn't it? What made you uncomfortable? When did you feel comfortable? How well are you working together as coleaders?

Integration of what has been happening in group sessions and theoretical perspectives on group stages, therapeutic factors, and leader interventions.

Planning for what needs to happen in the next session based on the previous levels of discussion. What are the goals for the group as a whole and each member individually? What content issues need to be addressed? What process issues need to be addressed? What needs to happen to help the group work together more productively? What needs to happen for individual members to work more productively? Specifically, who will do what and when?

Evaluation of what was helpful during the supervision session. What was helpful today? What did you learn? How did you learn it? What will you do differently next group session?

This format is intended to provide structure, reduce anxiety, and allow group leaders to reflect on what was helpful and not helpful, and plan for future group sessions. The use of written notes, such as DeLucia-Waack's (2002) planning and processing sheets, can be useful in this practice; these forms can be found in Appendices A and B.

Summary

Prior to beginning a group, much time must be spent organizing resources and planning topics and interventions. In addition, group leaders must prepare themselves personally and professionally for the type of group they will lead. Multicultural counseling considerations are also important as group leaders prepare for a group.

Learning Exercises

1. View a training DVD such as those listed below:

   - Bauman, S., & Steen, S. (2010). *Group counseling with children: A multicultural approach* [DVD]. Alexandria, VA: Association for Specialists in Group Work.
   - Bauman, S., & Steen, S. (2012). *Group counseling with adolescents: A multicultural approach* [DVD]. Alexandria, VA: Association for Specialists in Group Work.
   - Carroll, M. (1996). *Group work: Leading in the here and now* [DVD]. Alexandria, VA: Association for Specialists in Group Work.
   - Corey, M., Corey, G., & Hayes, R. (2004). *Evolution of groups* [DVD]. Belmont, CA: Brooks/Cole.
   - DeLucia-Waack, J. L., Segrist, A, Horne, A., & Nitza, A. (2006). *Leading groups with adolescent*s [DVD]. Alexandria, VA: Association for Specialists in Group Work.
   - Stockton, R. (1998). *Developmental aspects of group counseling* [DVD]. Alexandria, VA: Association for Specialists in Group Work.

   As you watch, identify examples of the skills described in this chapter as displayed by the group leaders. What category(ies) of skills are used most often? How do members seem to respond to the different skills used? Do the skills used change over the course of the group? What else do you observe?

2. Review the ASGW *Multicultural and Social Justice Competence Principles for Group Worke*rs (Singh et al., 2012). With a classmate, peer, or colleague, discuss the four steps posed by DeLucia-Waack and Donigian (2004), as listed on page 33 of this book. Which steps are most important for you to focus on currently as you plan your group? Which steps might you need to continue to explore in supervision and/or with your coleader?

6

Planning Group Sessions

Whether leading a counseling or psychoeducational group, the planning of group sessions is essential. Psychoeducational groups will have more structure, specifically around content and skill building, but structure is also important in counseling groups. All group sessions, regardless of type of group, should have a clear opening, working, processing, and ending component. This structure is essential to providing safety and continuity to group members. Structure is also necessary to manage time efficiently and focus on relevant issues (DeLucia-Waack, 2006).

Session Structure

Depending on the type of group and the age of group members, the level of structure may vary. The younger the group members are, the more structure is necessary. Psychoeducational groups tend to be more structured, with activities designed to facilitate discussion of a topic and/or development of new skills and behaviors. To make the transition from one group session to the next, it is helpful and creates a sense of trust when each group session has a structure that is expected and predictable.

Group sessions typically include four parts. The opening reviews material from a previous session, discusses homework efforts, and/or introduces the topic for the current session. The working part focuses on the goals of the group, allowing discussion and interaction around a specific topic or skill to identify, learn, and/or practice potentially effective behaviors. Processing activities typically include questions to help make sense of the working activities and apply them to life outside of group. Closing activities help group members prepare to leave group. Over the years, we have adapted this structure for counseling groups to use time efficiently, get all group members involved early in the session, and also develop a routine that facilitates safety for all group members.

Opening

At the beginning of a session, during the opening, structure focuses members on what they will need to discuss that day based on past sessions or new topics for the current session. If group members were asked to complete a task between group sessions, it is important to begin with a review of what they have done. The assignment typically is to practice a new behavior or coping strategy learned in the previous session or some kind of assignment in preparation for a new topic. It is useful to ask group members to review what they did with regard to this assignment and what they learned, and then use some focusing statements to direct toward the topic of the day.

Possible ways to begin sessions include check-ins or go-rounds that focus members on what they want to talk about and work on that day, review of homework from previous sessions, or reading of a poem or paragraph that relates to the issues previously discussed in the group or as an introduction to a new topic. For example, in an anger-management group, members might have been asked to identify situations where they felt irritated in the past week. The group leader may comment on some of the similarities expressed by the group members and then lead into a discussion of how to express irritation and other feelings in a way that will productively change the situation. To reinforce new strategies that have been learned in the previous week, group leaders may ask group members to identify one strategy they tried during the week, and if they did not try a strategy, when they might have tried one. Another technique that is helpful as part of the opening to lead into skills that will be practiced during the current session is to ask group members to write down on a piece of paper one situation during the past week that they could use help with. The papers are then crumpled, thrown in the middle of the circle, and redistributed so the situations are anonymous. Situations are then read aloud to emphasize universality and to identify potential skills needed and coping strategies, and they can be used later as a basis for role plays. General questions to open group sessions include the following:

- What did you do this week with what you learned in the previous session?
- Could we have a report on how you did with your homework assignments?
- What would you like to practice this week that you learned from last week?

Agenda setting for a team (Conyne, 2009) and previewing (Dye, 2006) are useful activities for opening sessions, as they help focus group members on what they need to accomplish during a session.

Working

For psychoeducational groups, the working part of the session is focused on discussion of skill building based on the goals of the group. Teaching and practicing of specific skills such as assertiveness, expression of feelings, and communication skills may be helpful in most psychoeducational groups, both to facilitate effective interactions in groups and to meet interpersonal group goals. In addition, techniques such as role-playing or Gestalt empty- or two-chair techniques may help develop new interpersonal skills and explore issues. Such techniques allow group members to explore and express feeling with others or to experience two sets of conflicting thoughts and feelings. For counseling groups, the focus is on working on group members' goals related to interpersonal issues. The content may not need to be predetermined, but skill building, practice, and role-playing situations will occur as needed to address group members' presenting topics for that day.

All groups with children and adolescents need to include interventions to discuss feelings, connect with others, and identify potential solutions for their concerns, regardless of the theme or topic of the group (DeLucia-Waack, 2006). These skills assist group members in identifying potential areas of strength and areas to work on, practice new skills, and learn content specific to group goals.

Children and adolescents often respond better to nonverbal techniques than to verbal exercises because of their limited vocabularies and disposition to display feelings through play. Creativity in activities, particularly singing, dancing, puppets, role plays, and music, is a way to identify and express feelings and to brainstorm and practice new behaviors and coping skills (DeLucia-Waack, 2006). Even adolescents who will initially remark that puppets or stuffed animals are silly or too young for them will often pick up one or more of these items and hold them. Techniques also need to focus on the development of new skills and serve as a reminder of when to implement them. How to choose activities, as well as suggestions for integrating them within sessions and processing them to promote learning, is the major focus of the rest of this book.

The majority of the focus of all three Association for Specialists in Group Work activity books (DeLucia-Waack, Bridbord, Kleiner, & Nitza, 2006; Foss, Green, Wolfe-Stiltner, & DeLucia-Waack, 2008; Salazar, 2009) is on activities to be used in the working part of a group session. "Stress Jenga" (Darst & Funke, 2006) focuses on coping skills to deal with stress, while "Fiddler on the Roof" (Horne, 2006) focuses on decision-making skills. "Level Playing Field" (Jackson, 2009) helps group members examine the impact of oppression and prejudice on all people, while "Hurting and Healing" (Bauman & Steen, 2009) emphasizes the power of discriminatory words and ways to heal those wounds. Bauman and Steen (2010) illustrate the use of that activity with fifth graders. "Are You Growing Worries" (Campbell, 2008) emphasizes the connection between thoughts and feelings and suggests coping strategies for anxiety, while "Up, Up, and Away" (Karcher, 2008) helps group members express feelings about people they have lost.

Some structure works well for older adolescents and counseling groups as well. Even for groups with more of a counseling focus, beginning each session with a short activity, maybe 10 to 15 minutes at the most, helps them generate some insight into their personal issues and perhaps introduces a framework within which to work on those issues. Completing a brief checklist of strengths or reading and then discussing a poem related to the group topic of the day helps focus the group members and prepares them to work on group and individual goals.

Processing

Processing is probably the most overlooked part of any group session but is particularly overlooked in psychoeducational groups. Some people will say that children are not capable of processing, while others will say that processing is unnecessary because in psychoeducational groups members are learning specific skills and the transfer of skills happens automatically. However, if one looks at the definition of processing, it becomes clear that processing is essential to the effectiveness of all groups, regardless of age, goals, or population. According to Stockton, Morran, and Nitza (2000), processing can be described as

> capitalizing on significant happenings in the here-and-now interactions of the group to help members reflect on the meaning of their experience, better understand their own thoughts, feelings and actions, and generalize what is learned to their life outside of the group. (p. 345)

Processing questions are intended to help members reflect on their reactions to the exercise, learn about themselves, and transfer their learning to their real lives.

Processing can be extremely useful in the teaching and application of specific skills related to the goals of a psychoeducational group. For example in a test anxiety group, discussing what it is like to speak in group allows group members to identify their source(s) of anxiety, perhaps normalize their anxiety if other members also share it, and begin to generate possible interventions for when anxiety occurs outside of group.

In addition, as part of ending the group session, it is important for group leaders to assess and reinforce what group members have learned from the group that day. Simply asking group members to identify what they have learned from the current session and how they will use it in the upcoming week helps ensure that the new information and skills are being integrated and applied. It was always amazing to us how clearly group members, even young children, could state what they learned from group that day. In addition, however, it was also comical, but perplexing to some extent, to hear comments that were tangential or did not seem to relate to the session at all. Thus, importance of clearly identifying what members have learned is emphasized. Processing is an important piece of each group session but takes a relatively small amount of time, maybe 3 to 8 minutes out of a 45- to 60-minute group. Some ways to process at the end of sessions include summaries (by leader, one member, or briefly by all), go-rounds of what each person has learned that day and/or thought was most helpful, brief written reactions given to the leader, and/or rating sheets. Go-rounds, such as the following, are often helpful at this time:

- What I learned from group today was . . .
- One thing that I will take from group today was . . .
- One new skill I will try out during the week will be . . .
- What, if anything, did you learn in today's session?
- What did you hear yourself or anyone else say that seemed especially significant to you?
- If you were to summarize the key themes that were explored today, what would they be?
- What was it like for you to be here today?

To emphasize altruism, role-modeling, and interpersonal learning, it is helpful to ask questions such as these:

- Who did you most connect with today and why?
- Each of you finish this sentence: "The thing I liked *best* (or least) about this session was _____."
- Who was most helpful to you today and why?
- Who did you learn the most from today, and what did you learn?
- Could we have everyone say what he or she is feeling right now?
- I like it when you _____.
- You had some different feelings during this session. What did you learn about yourself from this?

One of the most helpful parts of the three Association for Specialists in Group Work activity books (DeLucia-Waack et al., 2006; Foss et al., 2008; Salazar, 2009) is that each activity includes a list of possible processing questions to help make sense of the activity.

Questions that help identify what group members learned in group and how they helped others in group emphasize therapeutic factors and reinforce communication, problem solving, and social skills. Such questions might include the following:

- How did we work together today as a group?
- What did someone say or do today that was most helpful for you? What did you learn from it?

- What did we do as a group to generate new ideas? Try a new behavior? Learn something?
- What did you do today to help you learn something new?
- What did you do differently today in group?
- What did you do today to help someone else learn something?
- Does anyone want to give anyone else any feedback?
- Are there any changes you'd like to make in the group?
- What is each of you willing to say about each other's work?
- How is the group going for you so far?

Closing

At the end of a group session, structure helps clarify what has been learned. The closing part of the group session should also identify goals to work on between group sessions and help group members transition out of group. Recognizing that a group session is a small part of their week, it is essential to help members practice and apply outside of group what they have learned in group. Group members should leave the session with something to think about or practice before the next group session. Smead (1996) advocates inviting members, rather than requiring them, to try out new behaviors between group sessions if they are ready. General assignments to the whole group or a specific assignment to individual group members may be part of the closing. It is most helpful to involve group members in the development of the homework. Some ways to do this include asking group members to identify a specific situation during the week in which they will practice a skill they have learned; asking group members to identify one new behavior they will try out during the week; and asking group members to monitor a certain situation, feeling, or behavior during the week in anticipation of the next group session (e.g., identify situations where you compare yourself with others unfavorably).

- What would each of you like to do between now and the next session?
- Is there anything anyone wants to work on at the next session?
- I'd like to go around the group and have each of you complete this sentence: "One thing I need to practice outside of group is _____."
- Let's spend the last 10 minutes talking about your plans for the coming week. What is each of you willing to do outside of the group?
- What are you willing to do with the tension (or any other feeling) you feel?
- What will help you remember what you want to do differently?

- What can you do between now and the next session to practice what you've just learned?
- A homework assignment I'd like you to consider is _____.

It is also important to recognize that many uncomfortable feelings and thoughts may arise as a result of participation in a group session. This in and of itself is not bad, as people learn the most when they are a little uncomfortable. However, group members often need to leave group and return to their "real lives." For children and adolescents, this may mean going back to a class or some sport or social event where they have to interact with other students. Thus, it is important to include as part of the closing of a group session, some transitional element that helps group members leave some of the intense feelings and emotions in the room and transition back to their "real lives." Some kind of creative element or ritual is helpful here. Reading an inspirational poem or listening to music that is upbeat or soothing may be useful. Sometimes, playing music that the group members can dance to, to virtually shake off the negative emotions, is useful.

Care should be taken to plan interventions based on the goals, time allotted, and size of the group.

Session planning then involves identifying possible themes, interventions, and activities that group leaders might use to help each group member work on personal goals and interact in group. However, the specific content and order of topics and interventions will be decided as group members check in at the beginning of each session with what they want to work on during that group session.

Appendix A includes another more detailed outline of a planning sheet that helps group leaders plan each session in advance, organizing around the parts of each session—opening, working, processing, and closing—as well as identifying issues related to group members, goals, previous sessions, and group process. An example of a planning sheet for the eighth session of a children-of-divorce psychoeducational group is also included in Chapter 8, Case Example 1.

Summary

Thoughtful planning of group sessions is essential to the success of both psychoeducational and counseling groups. Each group session should have an opening, working part, processing, and closing section that has a clear focus and purpose. Effective session plans include time for an adequate opening and closing in addition to working time. Each activity or intervention should reflect the goals of that group session and match the needs and struggles inherent in each group stage.

Learning Exercises

1. View a group training DVD and identify the specific parts within a group session:

   - Opening
   - Working
   - Processing
   - Closing

   Possible group DVDs include the following:

   Bauman, S., & Steen, S. (2010). *Group counseling with children: A multicultural approach* [DVD]. Alexandria, VA: Association for Specialists in Group Work.
   Bauman, S., & Steen, S. (2012). *Group counseling with adolescents: A multicultural approach* [DVD]. Alexandria, VA: Association for Specialists in Group Work.
   Carroll, M. (1996). *Group work: Leading in the here and now* [DVD]. Alexandria, VA: Association for Specialists in Group Work.
   Corey, M., Corey, G., & Hayes, R. (2004). *Evolution of groups* [DVD]. Belmont, CA: Brooks/Cole.
   DeLucia-Waack, J. L., Segrist, A., Horne, A., & Nitza, A. (2006) *Leading groups with adolescents* [DVD]. Alexandria, VA: Association for Specialists in Group Work.
   Stockton, R. (1998). *Developmental aspects of group counseling* [DVD]. Alexandria, VA: Association for Specialists in Group Work.

2. Identify a group activity that could be used in the working session. Write processing questions that would help group members relate the activity to their group goals.

7

Planning Group Sessions

Whether leading a counseling or psychoeducational group, the planning of group sessions is essential. Selection of themes, interventions, goals, and activities must take into consideration the goal of the group, the format, the group stage, and target population.

_____ Outline and Content of Group Sessions

Once group leaders have identified typical goals and interventions specific to the type of group they plan to lead and have begun to select potential group members, it is time to begin to plan the content and order of the group sessions. Not all groups will focus on and/or accomplish all the goals that have been previously identified. The decision about which sessions to include must be based on the length of the group, the overall goals of the group, and individual needs of the group members. Psychoeducational groups in the schools, whether small groups or classroom guidance activities, should focus on teaching social skills and self-instructional models of thought and behavior change. Counseling groups will focus more on interpersonal relationships and specific difficulties group members are struggling with. This section describes how to choose activities and programmatic activities that address these two foci and also meet specific group goals. Care should be taken to plan interventions based on the goals, time allotted, and size of the group.

In psychoeducational groups, activities are an essential part of the group structure to teach and practice new behaviors and skills. Group leaders tailor activities to the main task inherent in the current group stage and overall group goals. From the very beginning of the first group session, all group activities, processing of group activities, and group discussions should emphasize group goals and norms such as self-disclosure, self-exploration, and feedback as they relate to the facilitation of group goals. The chapters that follow describe the four stages of group, discuss main tasks and foci of each stage, and suggest potential interventions and activities.

When designing a psychoeducational group, there are a variety of materials and resources to choose from. There are fully developed treatment modules for specific types of groups that leaders may follow step by step; resources that include outlines for individual group sessions that address certain goals; and also books, games, videos, and other materials that may be utilized within a group session. This section first discusses how to choose and sequence group sessions that will meet the goals of a specific psychoeducational group, taking into consideration age of group members, treatment length, and individual needs of group members. First, an outline is described that will aid in selecting group sessions.

Planning for counseling group sessions is equally as important as planning for sessions in psychoeducational groups, but with a different emphasis. While psychoeducational groups will have a clear outline of what group leaders want to accomplish in particular order, group leaders of counseling groups must obtain a clear understanding of the interpersonal aspects of members' presenting problems as well as a rationale for how the mechanisms of change to be utilized in the group will be used to address members' relational goals (Whittingham, 2013). The use of assessment tools such as the CORE-R Battery (Burlingame et al., 2006) and the Group Readiness Questionnaire (Burlingame, Davies, Cox, Baker, Beecher, & Gleave, 2010) during group screening can assist leaders in identifying and targeting the precise interpersonal difficulties members are struggling with and how these difficulties are likely to play out in the context of the group. This information can then be used to "establish clear treatment goals, maintain a focus on those goals, provide active and efficient leadership, and maintain a here and now focus" (Whittingham, 2013, p. 16).

Session planning then involves identifying possible themes, interventions, and activities that they might use to help each group member work on their goal and interact in group. However, the specific content and order of topics and interventions will be decided as group members check in at the beginning of each group session with what they want to work on that day.

Matching Sessions to Group Goals

It is important to decide the sequence and contents of each group session prior to the onset of a group, because so much of what happens in group is interconnected. For instance, in screening interviews, preparation sessions, and the first session, it is useful to describe group goals, typical group topics and themes, and interventions that will be used. Thus, those decisions need to be made ahead of time. In addition, any homework assigned during a session should lead logically into the topic and interventions that will occur in the following sessions. Moreover, it is important for group leaders to plan for the sessions in advance and gather group materials.

A general guideline for planning a psychoeducational group should be at least one session each for both opening and termination sessions, and one to two sessions focused on each goal. Generally, an 8-week psychoeducational group should have two to three goals. It would then be possible to spend 5 to 6 weeks on the content to meet those two to three goals. Conyne (2003) suggested a model for skill acquisition that recommends most skills be addressed in more than one session.

The model is as follows:

- Present content to be learned.
- Describe relevant skill.
- Demonstrate skill.
- Practice, perhaps in pairs.
- Give performance feedback.
- Discuss application to real-world settings.
- Retry skill.
- Hold general processing discussion with entire group.

Goals should generally focus on changing or teaching new skills and behavior in three areas: affect, cognition, and behavior. Affect focuses on the feelings elicited, with the general goals of psychoeducational groups being increasing positive affect and decreasing negative affect. Cognitions include both maladaptive and adaptive thoughts that group members think about themselves, the people they interact with, and the situations they are involved in. General goals of psychoeducational groups related to cognitions include the identification, generation of, and reinforcement of positive thoughts that help the group members try out new behaviors and feel good about themselves. Another goal related to cognitions in psychoeducational groups is identification and disputing of irrational beliefs that make group members feel depressed, bad about themselves, or interfere with social skills. Behavioral goals for psychoeducational groups include teaching of skills related to expression of feelings, communication skills, conflict-management skills, stress-management skills, and relationship skills. It is a good idea to include one goal from each of the three categories as general goals for psychoeducational groups. For example, in a social skills group, the affective goal might be identification of negative feelings in social situations, the cognitive goal might be identification of the thoughts that make the student feel bad in social situations, and the behavioral goal might be the teaching and practicing of how to introduce yourself to new people.

Appendix C includes a planner for an eight-session group. The idea is to list for each session the session number, topic, title, interventions to be used, and homework to be assigned, along with space to make notes after each group session. Appendix A includes another more detailed outline of a planning sheet that helps group leaders plan each session in advance, organizing around the parts of each session—opening, working, processing, and closing—as well as identifying issues related to group members, goals, previous sessions, and group process. An example of a planning sheet for an eighth session of a children-of-divorce psychoeducational group is also included in Chapter 8, Case Example 1.

To decide which sessions should be included in a specific psychoeducational group, it is necessary to go back and compare what literature suggests as important goals, topics, and interventions with the needs of potential group members and the setting in which the group is to be conducted. Appendix D includes a grid that helps systematically organize group goals and interventions suggested in the literature (and by other practitioners) as a backdrop to plan a specific group. Once common group goals for a particular group are apparent, based on the literature and current group practice, group leaders can choose which goals this particular group will focus on.

Matching Interventions and Activities to Session Topics

Once group leaders have identified goals for a specific group, it is important to survey the literature to see what interventions are suggested to meet those goals and also what specific group sessions have already been designed to incorporate the interventions to achieve those goals. It does not make sense to reinvent the wheel every time a group leader starts a new group. This is probably one of the biggest deterrents to leading groups, particularly psychoeducational groups. Psychoeducational groups, as is probably evident by now, take a great deal of time to plan and examine the literature—a luxury most group leaders do not have. Thus, it is important to identify resources such as those by Morganett and Smead, the three Association for Specialists in Group Work activity books, the Association for Specialists in Group Work training DVDs, and others noted throughout this book so that interventions already shown to be effective can be used, necessitating creation only of those interventions and activities not yet designed. The first column in the grid in Appendix D lists group goals gathered from the literature and counseling practice. The second column lists interventions suggested to meet the goals for this particular type of psychoeducational group. The third column identifies group sessions already designed to meet specific group goals. Now it is time to examine the grid: What goals have corresponding interventions and sessions designed to meet them? Which do not? These will be the goals that need interventions and group sessions created for them, including goals, activities, and processing questions. The idea here is to see what is already out there and then add to the literature with new group sessions for the given type of group.

For example, a group leader may decide to use the second and third sessions of an anger-management group by Morganett (1990) because the interventions outlined in the sessions meet the goals of the particular group being led. Or someone may choose to use the Kid's Grief Kit (LeGrand, 2006) as part of a grief group to help children identify the different stages of grief. Appendix D illustrates the use of the literature and local resources to identify specific interventions and entire group sessions that may be used in a grief group.

Session planning for counseling groups can be done by considering relevant relational themes to be discussed, as well as by identifying interventions to be utilized as process issues related to members' interpersonal difficulties arise in the here and now of the sessions. Leaders can use ongoing formative assessment to further inform session planning. Group process and dynamics can be assessed by using instruments such as the Group Climate Questionnaire (MacKenzie, 1981) or the Critical Incident Questionnaire (Kivlighan & Goldfine, 1991). Whittingham (2013) recommends that group members' progress toward their interpersonal goals be assessed using the Outcome Questionnaire (Wells, Burlingame, Lambert, & Hope, 1996) or the Inventory of Interpersonal Problems–32 (Horowitz, Alden, Wiggins, & Pincus, 2000). Processing notes (see Appendix B) at the end of each session are also useful in tracking important individual and group-as-a-whole dynamics to be addressed in subsequent sessions. Many of the resources described previously in this chapter can be useful in identifying activities to address specific interpersonal goals within counseling groups. However, as cautioned by Yalom (2005), an overreliance on structured activities can detract from the here-and-now group process that is the primary mechanism of change in counseling and therapy groups.

Matching Interventions and Sessions to Group Stages

One of the initial tasks inherent in group work is to choose an activity appropriate for the stage of the group you are working through. According to Yalom (2005), structured activities, when appropriately chosen, can serve to accelerate the group past a particularly slow or stuck phase of the group. Following the framework postulated by Jones and Robinson (2000), activities should be chosen based on the following three stages: initial, working, and ending. Group leaders should tailor activities to the main task or issue inherent in the stage the group is currently working through. They also suggest that intensity should be a key determinant in the choice of an activity by stage. They define intensity as

the extent to which the group topic, structured exercises, and group techniques do the following: (a) evoke anxiety among the group participants, (b) challenge group participants to self-disclose, (c) increase awareness, (d) focus on feelings, (e) concentrate on the here and now, and (f) focus on threatening issues. (p. 358)

Initial-stage activities should focus on building trust and introducing members to the group and to each other. Working-stage activities should focus on helping members self-disclose, become involved in the process of group, and learn new behavioral and thought patterns to meet group goals. Ending activities should focus on assisting the members in termination and putting to use what they have learned once the group has ended. Thus, the chosen activity should focus on overcoming obstacles that are inherent in each respective stage.

Initial Stage

Activities used during the initial stage of the group should focus on help-ing members introduce themselves to the group, meet their fellow members, and overcome their anxiety (Jones & Robinson, 2000). This stage is charac-terized by encouraging interactions that are of low intensity and focus on orienting members to the norms, processes, and interactions of the group. These activities should involve minimal affective components and should be nonthreatening. The focus should be on decreasing, rather than increasing, the members' anxiety. As members tend to feel anxious and relatively unwill-ing to disclose, activities should parallel this constraint on interaction. Choosing an activity that focuses on high levels of disclosure and affect would be too intense and threatening for members at this stage. Typical activities focus on introductions, trust building, and modeling appropriate behavior. Examples of activities for the initial stage include "Autobiography" (Bridbord, 2006), "Guess Who?" (Doughty, 2006), "Elephant in the Room" (Becerra, 2009), "You're One Unique Cookie" (Leddick, 2009), "Risk Bag" (Coventry, 2008), "Millions of Families" (Erguner-Tekinalp, 2008), and "Looking at Process" (Brown, 2006).

Middle Stage

The middle stage of group is characterized by intense affect, increased self-disclosure, and an accelerated willingness to work on one's own issues. As the group moves past the initial conflicts of safety and trust, a higher sense of cohesion develops, allowing for increased self-exploration and expression. Thus, members are more willing to take risks with the activities presented. Subsequently, activities chosen for this stage of group should be of high intensity. That is, these activities should encourage members to increase their self-awareness; increase affective involvement; take risks and try out new behaviors, skills, and attitudes; and work through personal issues that may interfere with trying out new behaviors and skill sets. Activities for this stage of group should be challenging for the members, as well as anxiety provoking. Through this, members will be assisted in contributing the appropriate amount of disclosure within the group. More intense activities will match the group members' increased willingness and eagerness to explore new ways of thinking and behaving. Activities at this stage might also assist members in working with conflict, recognizing a wider range of emotions and expressions, and focusing on the here and now. Activities that can be used during the working stage of group include "A Group Image" (N. Brown, 2006), "Our Two Faces" (Gerrity, 2006), "We Live Under the Same Sky" (Erguner-Tekinalp, 2008), "Identifying Your Family Role" (Abram, 2008), "Strategies to Prevent Cultural–Racial Prejudice" (D'Andrea & Daniels, 2009), and "My Multiple Heritage Identity" (Henriksen & Paladino, 2009b).

Ending Stage

Activities that are chosen for the ending stage of group should focus on issues surrounding termination. In light of impending termination, members should move away from the high-intensity encounters and focus on the integration and application of new skills and attitudes. Thus, activities selected for this stage should focus on exploring what the members have gained from the group and how it will impact their lives in the future. Activities could also focus on helping the members say goodbye to each other and express what they have learned and gained from each other. Activities should be less intense than in the working stage and should focus on helping members achieve closure from the group. Examples of activities that are appropriate for the termination stage of group include "Closing: Thanking Others" (DeLucia-Waack, 2006), "Closing: What Have We Learned About Ourselves" (DeLucia-Waack, 2006), "My Core Self: The Center of the Quilt" (Thomas, 2006), and "Feedback as Poetry" (Wilson, 2006).

Summary

Thoughtful planning of group sessions is essential to the success of both psychoeducational and counseling groups. A group outline based on both individual and group goals can be used as a foundation from which individual sessions are designed, using the level of structure appropriate for the type of group being conducted. Session topics should be carefully sequenced, taking into consideration group goals and stages of group development. The selection of appropriate interventions and activities centers on the session topic, the stage of the group, and the specific needs of group members. Each activity should match the needs and struggles inherent in each group stage. One final consideration for selecting an activity that is appropriate for the group centers on the demographic characteristics of the group. It is important to choose an activity appropriately matched to the age level of the group. If this care is not taken, young group members may be faced with an activity that is too advanced for their understanding, while older group members may perceive the activity as not sophisticated enough for their maturity level.

Learning Exercises

1. Choose a group topic and conduct a literature search on that topic. Complete the "Grid for Choosing Sessions Based on Current Research and Practice" (Appendix D). Decide what sessions you need to design based on the gaps in your grid.

2. Once you have chosen your group goals, session topics, and interventions and activities, complete the "Eight-Session Group Planner" (Appendix C).

8

Case Examples in Planning a Group

Case Example 1: Planning and Designing a Psychoeducational Group for Children of _____ Divorce for Second and Third Graders

Group Goals

Reasonable goals for a 12-week children-of-divorce (COD) group for second and third graders include gaining an accurate picture of the divorce process, normalizing common experiences and feelings related to divorce, and providing a safe and supportive place to talk about divorce-related concerns. See the session planner below for a summary of goals and interventions selected to address those goals.

Gender Mix and Group Size

Crespi et al. (2005) suggest that a mixed group "offers opportunities to clarify and teach students about gender and relational dynamics" (p. 73); so it was decided to include second- and third-grade boys and girls.

Length and Number of Sessions

Since 30 to 40 minutes is optimal with children between 6 and 9 years old, a 40-minute group session was selected. Since standard programs are 12 to 14 sessions (e.g., Pedro-Caroll & Cowen, 1985; Stolberg & Cullen, 1985), a 12-week group was chosen with support from teachers and administrators.

Choosing the Content of Sessions

Depending on the individual needs of the children, the content sessions in the middle of the group might focus on

- discussion of the family situation (e.g., living arrangements, custody, visitation, extended family, other support);
- definition of important legal terms (e.g., *separation, divorce, custody, courts*) and information about divorce;
- identification and evaluation of worries and beliefs—specifically, magical thinking and irrational beliefs about the divorce (e.g., "I'll never see my father again," "I can get my parents back together again," "We'll be homeless," "My dad left me so my mom may leave me too," "It is my fault that they got divorced");
- expression of feelings about the divorce (e.g., anger, sadness, grief, loneliness, relief);
- solutions to problems generated by problem solving around difficult situations (e.g., visitation, new parental relationships, parental fighting, parental dating, blended families, stepparents, stepsiblings); and
- development of skills to deal with difficult situations (e.g., communication, conflict resolution, anger management, expression of feelings).

The Initial Assessment Instrument (Beech Acres Airing Institute, 1993, as cited in DeLucia-Waack, 2001) assessed potential concerns in the following areas: the divorce experience, parental fighting, legal aspects of the divorce, feelings of being caught in the middle, how to maintain parental relationships, changes since the divorce, parents' new partners, stepfamilies, traditions and holidays, and future family plans. The Children's Beliefs About Parental Divorce Scale (Kurdek & Berg, 1987) assessed irrational beliefs related to the divorce: fear of peer ridicule, avoidance, paternal blame, fear of abandonment, hope of reunification, and self-blame.

Group Leader Preparation

Coleadership for a COD group is preferable (DeLucia-Waack, 2011). The benefits of coleadership are two role models, two leaders who can cooperate and work together, and two sets of eyes and ears to observe the content and process of the group. In addition, for COD groups, a male–female coleadership team can model collaboration between male and female adults and provide contact with supportive and caring adults of both sexes. A male presence in the group is particularly important, because many of the children may not have much contact with a male adult, especially in an elementary school setting (Kalter, 1998).

To prepare for the group, leaders need to think about it from several different perspectives. How will they personally and professionally prepare for the group? How will they prepare others for the group—specifically, their school or agency (including administrators), parents, and children? As leaders begin to get ready for a COD group, they need to have a sense of their beliefs about divorce, the needs of children of divorce, and how a group can best help them. To do this, they first must examine their own personal values and experiences with divorce and separation. Second, they must examine current literature about what is most effective with these children in terms of themes, interventions, structure, and so forth. To begin to establish trust and cooperation as coleaders, they should meet regularly before the group starts to discuss theoretical orientation, leadership style, and goals and interventions for the group. Each coleader should assess his or her strengths and weaknesses as a leader of the particular COD group he or she is planning.

Evaluation

The Critical Incidents Questionnaire (Kivlighan & Goldfine, 1991) was used to assess group process and important therapeutic factors for each group member during a specific group session. The Revised Children's Manifest Anxiety Scale (Reynolds & Richmond, 1985), the Children's Depression Inventory (Kovacs, 1992; normed specifically on children of divorce), and the Children's Beliefs About Parental Divorce Scale (Kurdek & Berg, 1987) were used to assess changes in anxiety, depression, and concerns about divorce.

12-Session Group Planner

Session #	Topic*	Session Title
Session 1	Introduction	Introduction to Each Other and to the Group
Session 2	Introduction	Lots of Children Have Parents Who Are Divorced
Session 3	The divorce experience	How Divorce Happened in My Family
Session 4	The divorce experience	What Are Our Families Like?
Session 5	The divorce experience	Our Families and Friends: Who Can We Talk To?
Session 6	Feelings	Feelings About the Divorce
Session 7	Feelings	The Emotional Process of Divorce
Session 8	The divorce experience	Is It My Fault?
Session 9	Legal aspects	What Do All the Big Words Mean for Me?
Session 10	Changes	Life Is Tough, and Some Ways to Cope With It
Session 11	Ending	Ending
Session 12	Ending	What Have I Learned From This Group?

Planning Sheet for Session 8 _____

Date: 10/12   *Session #:* 8   *Group Leaders:*

Members already excused   Sandra (told us last week that she has a
                               doctor's appt.)

Check in With . . .

*Members who need to be checked in with who didn't finish working on
an issue last week*: Tommy still didn't think he could tell his dad to stop
asking him to relay messages to his mom.

*Members who were given an assignment or were going to report back this
week*: Kristin was going to talk to her older sister about her feelings about
the divorce.

Other members who might need to be checked in with and about what:
Justin was very quiet last session.

Group Topics or Issues to Be Finished and/or Revisited

Related to individual member or group goals: Check in on how members
expressed their feelings during the week.

Related to group process: How to let each person have some time to talk.

Group Topics or Issues to Be Addressed for the First Time

Content issues that need to be addressed for the first time: How to deal
with parents' new relationships.

Process issues that need to be addressed for the first time: Members being
quiet for a whole session.

Specific Interventions

Session _____

I Tried to Get My Mom and
Dad Back Together Again _____

from DeLucia-Waack (2001)

Materials

Banner with group name and ground rules hanging on the wall

If You Believe in You tape (specifically, the "I Tried" song)

A large notepad with markers

Group Session

Review and Check-In (7 minutes)

1. Play the "I Tried" song (3 minutes).

2. What's the song about? Emphasize how hard it is to meet the new boyfriend or girlfriend when parents start dating and how most children of divorce want their parents to get back together again (4 minutes).

Working Activities (30 minutes)

3. *Getting My Parents Back Together* (5 minutes). Today, we are going to talk about the idea that just about everyone wants his or her parents to get back together. Let's start by talking about why this is so. Why do children want both of their parents to live in the same house?

4. *When My Parents Lived Together* (10 minutes). Now let's try to remember what it was like when both parents did live in the same house. (If some of the children don't remember, ask them to think about what it is like when their parents spend time together now.) Let's make a list of the good things and the not-so-good things about parents being together. Use the large notepad to record two columns: "Good Things" and "Not-So-Good Things." (Leave room between the columns so you can add two more columns later.)

5. *How Would It Be Different?* (5 minutes). Now let's work on both of those lists one at a time. Let's first talk about the "Not-So-Good Things" list. How would those be different if your parents got back together now? Do you think they would change? (Emphasize that parents would probably still fight and argue about the same things, because they are still different people.)

6. *Good Things and How to Make Them Happen* (10 minutes). Now let's work on the list of "Good Things." Let's add another column called "How to Make the Good Things Happen Now." How can this happen now? Let's brainstorm ways to make this happen. Let's also identify things that can't happen and maybe suggest other things that can take their place (e.g., Sunday dinner with Mom and Dad being replaced with Sunday dinner with Mom and her family).

Processing (5 minutes)

7. When families change, some good things happen and some bad things happen. Let's everyone go around and finish the sentence, "*One good thing that can still happen in my family is _____.*"

Closing (3 minutes)

8. Let's listen to "I Tried" again. Feel free to sing along. Let's listen to the message at the end: "I let go and stopped trying to get my parents back together again."

Other Issues/Topics to Be Addressed

This is our last session to talk about new issues and strategies; termination sessions begin next week.

Issues to Be Discussed With Supervisor

How to introduce termination without taking too much time but getting the children to start thinking about what they have learned and what they can do outside of group.

Group Processing Sheet for 10-Session COD Group _____

Group Process Notes _____

Date: 10/13	Session #: 8	Group Leaders: J & T
Members Present:	Members Excused:	Members Not Excused:

Tommy, Justin, Kristin, Sandy

Susan, Andy

Themes for the Group

Content: How kids try to get their parents back together again

Sadness over the divorce

Good things that happen now that parents are divorced
Process: It's hard to talk about feelings.

Notes for the Group

Opening: Listened to "I Tried." Talked about how Kelly and Cory didn't like their parents' new boyfriends and girlfriends.

Working: Came up with several reasons why children want their parents in the same house: to see both of them, to be a family, to get love from both of them. Made lists of "Good Things" and "Not-So-Good Things" about parents being together and then talked about how things from the "Not-So-Good Things" list would/would not change if their parents got back together. Tommy and Justin started by saying that things would be different and their parents wouldn't fight anymore. But then Susan pointed out that her parents still fight when they are living apart, so she didn't think it would change if they lived together again. Shifted the discussion to how to make the good things happen now. Susan suggested that her parents could both still come to her soccer game but didn't need to sit with each other. Tommy said he could have a special dinner with Mom once a week, just she and him, like they used to. Others talked about how they could ask to do things with their father that they had stopped doing because they didn't live together, like helping with homework, washing the car, or taking walks.

Ending: Everyone took a turn and stated, "One good thing that can still happen in my family is . . . ." Answers focused on spending time with both parents. Sang "I Tried."

Notes About Each Group Member

Andy: Really wanted to believe that his parents wouldn't fight anymore and could get back together again.

Justin: Still quiet but did talk and had some good ideas about stuff that he could do with his family right now, particularly his dad.

Kristin: Wants her parents back together but not if they will fight.

Sandy: Excused.

Susan: Seems to have accepted that her parents are divorced; doesn't like that they still argue now. Was going to talk to her mom about things they could do together.

Tommy: Was quiet at the beginning when talking about parents' boyfriends or girlfriends; laughed really hard about spilling wine on her dress. Says mom doesn't date now.

Processing of the Group Session

Comments About the Group

Content: Lots of talk about what was bad when parents were together, but hard to make suggestions to make it good now.

Process: Laughed a lot about not liking parents' new boyfriends and girl-friends. Had a hard time at first coming up with good things that happened after the divorce, but then were able to.

Specific members: Justin talked more this session.

To be discussed in supervision: How to get them all to talk more about their feelings

Evaluation of Intervention Strategies

Executive Functions

What worked: Starting on time

What didn't (and what you could do differently next time): Trying to nonverbally get Tommy to stop tapping his pencil (sit next to him)

Meaning Attribution

What worked: Asking them what was different now so that their parents wouldn't fight anymore if they got back together

What didn't (and what you could do differently next time): Asking them if they had similar feelings to those of Kelly and Cory about their parents' boyfriends and girlfriends (ask them how Kelly and Cory might act out their feelings)

Caring

What worked: Saying yes, this is tough to talk about sometimes, and then asking for a group hug

What didn't (and what could you do differently next time): Asking them to say what is tough at the end

Emotional Stimulation

What worked: I don't think I did anything to do this, this time.

What didn't (and what you could do differently next time):

Critical Incidents Related to Therapeutic Factors

(Instillation of hope, universality, imparting of information, altruism, the corrective recapitulation of the primary family group, interpersonal learning—input, interpersonal learning—output, cohesiveness, catharsis, existential factors, identification, self-understanding.) Briefly describe the three most critical incidents that happened this week in group and how each illustrates a therapeutic factor.

1. Instillation of hope when Susan said that she had hoped for a long time that her parents would stop fighting and it didn't happen, but she focuses on how much each of them loves her and that makes her feel better.

2. Universality when all the members said that sometimes they wished their parents would get back together again.

3. Imparting of information when I said that it is normal to want your parents back together; most children do, and they are sad when it doesn't happen.

Countertransference

Toward Specific Members

Briefly describe the feeling toward the member, who the person reminds you of (if any), and how you behave toward the member based on this. Is your reaction based on something that a person is doing in group or on assumptions you are making about the person based on relationships with others? What could you do in the future to respond to this person as he or she is in the group and not as if this person were someone else?

1. I don't feel very connected to Justin because it is so hard to know what he is thinking since he is so quiet and doesn't display many nonverbals. I am trying to engage him more to see what he does think and whom he is like as a person.

2. Susan reminds me of myself when I was young—wanting very much for everything to be OK and to connect with all members of her family. I probably support her more than others because of this, so I need to watch and make sure that I don't smooth things over to make them OK for her but do support her efforts to connect with others.

Toward Specific Incidents or Group Topics

Briefly describe the event, the feeling(s) elicited from you as a result of the event, what other situation this reminds you of, what behavior it is based on, what your personal reactions and issues are related to this event, and what you can do differently in future interactions.

1. It is hard to listen to the children say that they want their parents back together when I know rationally that it was probably a pretty uncomfortable situation for a lot of them. I want to fix it for them and may

rush in too soon. I need to step back, help them discuss and process feelings, and come to their own conclusions.

Case Example 2: Planning and Designing a Counseling Group for a University Counseling Center

Group Goals

The following case example is adapted from Focused Brief Group Therapy (FBGT; Whittingham, 2012). FBGT is an evidenced-based, semi-structured, brief integrative model. It was developed over six years in a university counseling center and has been manualized (Whittingham and Lotz, 2012) to aid in training and supervision. Early research on the approach found statistically and clinically significant change for students in a mean of 6.5 sessions on depression, social anxiety, hostility and interpersonal distress (Rotsinger-Stemen & Whittingham, 2013).

This counseling group is designed to address the interpersonal difficulties that college students face in dealing with the transition to, and demands of, the college environment. Many of the developmental tasks that college students face are rooted in interpersonal concerns. Therefore, the broad goals of this process-oriented group are to facilitate or strengthen skills in attaching to others, managing interpersonal difficulties, and developing more flexible interpersonal styles and strategies.

From within this framework, the group targets specific, achievable individual goals for members based on changing behaviors that cause interpersonal distress. By accurately establishing the *precise* area of interpersonal distress for each member (using the screening and evaluation processes described below) and generating behavioral goals related to creating interpersonal flexibility in that area, members are assisted in moving purposefully toward meaningful change.

Length and Number of Sessions

This group is designed as an 8-week group to operate within the logistical constraints of a college counseling center that operates on a 10-week quarter system. To best utilize the group process as the mechanism of change with this young adult population, sessions are 90 minutes in length.

Screening and Selection

Screening and selection are essential to the success of this group to maximize goal achievement in the brief time frame available. The primary emphasis of screening is a focused assessment of problems with interpersonal functioning. The Inventory of Interpersonal Problems–32 (IIP–32; Horowitz, Alden, Wiggins, & Pincus, 2000) is used in combination with an interpersonal screening interview. The IIP–32 is based on the interpersonal circumplex (first used by Leary, 1957), which captures personality along two basic dimensions—agency (control, dominance, or power) and affiliation (also referred to as agreeableness). The agency dimension is an axis from dominant to submissive, while the affiliation dimension is an axis from friendly to hostile. All other points on the circumplex are a combination of these two components.

Combined with the IIP–32 results, an interpersonal interview is used to determine what relational patterns exist for the client that may impact his or her global functioning. By asking questions about interpersonal history with friends, family, romantic partners, and work/school friends, it is possible to establish patterns that become visible to the client. Once insight is gained into problems with relationships and how they impact functioning, they are able to understand the roots of their current symptom distress and more accurately understand the work they need to do.

Inclusion/exclusion criteria are centered on the importance of heterogeneity of interpersonal style as an important facet of interpersonal process groups. The IIP–32 results are thus used to select a heterogeneous group membership to maximize interpersonal learning toward goal achievement. Ideally, members should represent the range of styles within the interpersonal circumplex; the presence of too many members with any one interpersonal style might result in a group that gets "stuck" and limits opportunities for growth. Additional exclusion criteria included symptoms or situational concerns that would prevent the individual from participating in a meaningful way in the central tasks of the group. These include current severe crises, the presence of current alcohol or substance dependence, and individuals who have a rigid externalizing style (e.g., somaticization).

Selecting the Content of Sessions

As described above, goals for the group are focused on interpersonal behaviors related to creating a more flexible interpersonal style for members. After having identified precise areas of interpersonal distress, goals are collaboratively developed that should be measurable and achievable within the time-limited group structure. The emphasis is on increasing the range of behavioral options available to each individual. For example, a goal for a member struggling with social inhibition might be to initiate a conversation at least twice throughout the group.

As a counseling group, sessions are not as structured or content focused as in a psychoeducational group; much of the work takes place as leaders respond to significant events as they occur in the here-and-now process of the group. However, leaders are guided by a clear understanding of each member's interpersonal style and goals and a set of techniques for promoting work toward these goals. Having preassessed members' interpersonal styles, the active ingredients in group are steered toward members' presenting problems. Among the techniques to be used are (1) maintaining a clear goal focus using active reminders and inviting individuals to take steps toward their goals, (2) combining the work of members with complementary styles and goals, (3) process illumination, and (4) facilitating feedback loops that are directed toward specific areas of interpersonal distress. Interventions might include statements such as "Carmen, it seems like one of your goals, of reaching out to someone empathically, just got met. What was that like?" An additional intervention might be, "Trey, it seems like it was hard for you to empathize with Mark just then. I wonder if you would like to practice working on that right now?" A feedback loop can be encouraged by asking one member to give feedback to another member working on difficulty exhibiting warmth. The feedback might involve sharing that he or she sometimes feels not cared for by this person and would really like it if the person showed that he or she cared by demonstrating active listening.

Leader Preparation

Coleadership is preferable for this interpersonally focused counseling group. In addition to allowing one leader to observe the group process while the other facilitates discussion, the relationship between the coleaders serves as an important source of modeling and learning for members. To be prepared to colead effectively, both leaders should complete the IIP–32 themselves to establish an understanding of their own styles and how they are likely to interact with each other and as a part of the overall group dynamic. Questions to be considered and discussed based on the assessment results include *What is my go-to interpersonal style? What kind of leadership style do I have based on that? Who am I likely to be activated by in a group? Who are we together? What are our strengths and deficits as a team, and how should we adapt accordingly?*

Additionally, leaders should be well prepared by understanding the premises behind the interpersonal approach to group work and have a good understanding of the measures used to assess interpersonal style to accurately interpret members' scores and help them develop appropriate group goals. Finally, leaders should be able to balance relational and structuring skills to facilitate group cohesion and a positive group dynamic while also promoting progress toward goals. This includes being warm, collaborative, and culturally sensitive while also maintaining a focus on individual goals and challenging members as appropriate.

Evaluation

Both process and outcome evaluation are important to this counseling group. Process measures used include the Group Climate Questionnaire–Short Form (MacKenzie, 1983) and the Working Alliance Inventory (Horvath & Greenberg, 1989). Together, these two instruments can be used to track members' connection to or engagement with the group, as well as their goal directedness and sense that the group is accomplishing its tasks. These measures can be used in the early and middle stages of the group (e.g., in this eight-session group, they can be used after Sessions 2 and 5), and adjustments can be made based on the results as necessary.

Outcome measurement is achieved by using the IIP–32 as a pre–post assessment of change. An additional pre–post outcome assessment is the Counseling Center Assessment of Psychological Symptoms (Sevig et al., 2006), which is a self-report measure of university student functioning that captures college-related distress in areas such as academic functioning, social anxiety, depression, and family problems. The combination of these two measures allows for a thorough assessment of both symptomatic and behavioral change to determine the effectiveness of the group.

Appendix A _____
Group Planning Sheet

DeLucia-Waack (2002)

Date: Session #:   Group Leaders:

Members already excused:

Check in With . . .

Members who need to be checked in with who didn't finish working on an issue last week:

Members who were given an assignment or were going to report back this week:

Other members who might need to be checked in with and about what:

Group Topics or Issues That Need to Be Finished and/or Revisited

Related to individual member or group goals:

Related to group process:

Group Topics or Issues to
Be Addressed for the First Time

Content issues that need to be addressed for the first time:

Process issues that need to be addressed for the first time:

Specific Interventions

Opening:
Processing:
Closing:

Other Issues/Topics to Be Addressed

Issues to Be Discussed in Supervision

Appendix B _____

Group Processing Sheet

DeLucia-Waack (2002)

_____**Group Process Notes**

Date: Session #:   Group Leaders:

Members Present: Members Excused: Members Not Excused:

Themes for the Group

Content:

Process:

Notes for the Group

Opening:

Working:

Ending:

Notes About Each Group Member

Member A:

Member B:

Member C:

Member D:

Member E:

Member F:

(This ends what should be included in a group notes file and/or a client file. For a client file, include all the notes up to this point and then just the notes in the last section for that particular group member.)

Processing of the Group Session _____

Comments About the Group

Content:

Process:

Specific members:

To be discussed in supervision:

Evaluation of Intervention Strategies

Executive Functions

What worked:

What didn't (and what you could do differently next time):

Meaning Attribution

What worked:

What didn't (and what you could do differently next time):

Caring

What worked:

What didn't (and what you could do differently next time):

Emotional Stimulation

What worked:

What didn't (and what you could do differently next time):

Critical Incidents Related to Therapeutic Factors:

(Instillation of hope, universality, imparting of information, altruism, the corrective recapitulation of the primary family group, interpersonal learning—input, interpersonal learning—output, cohesiveness, catharsis, existential factors, identification, self-understanding.) Briefly describe the three most critical incidents that happened this week in group and how each illustrates a therapeutic factor.

1.

2.

3.

Now name the critical incident for each group member and what therapeutic factor it illustrates.

Member A:

Member B:

Member C:

Member D:

Member E:

Member F:

Member G:

Member H:

Countertransference

Toward Specific Members

Briefly describe the feeling toward the member, who the person reminds you of (if any), and how you behave toward the member based on this. Is your reaction based on something that a person is doing in group or on assumptions you are making about the person based on relationships with others? What could you do in the future to respond to this person as he or she is in the group and not as if this person were someone else?

1.

2.

Toward Specific Incidents or Group Topics

Briefly describe the event, the feeling(s) elicited from you as a result of the event, what other situation this reminds you of, what behavior it is based on, what your personal reactions and issues are related to this event, and what you can do differently in future interactions.

1.

2.

Appendix C _____

Eight-Session Group Planner

Session #	Topic*	Session Title
Session 1:		Introduction
Interventions:		
Notes:		
Homework:		
Session 2:		Introduction
Interventions:		
Notes:		
Homework:		
Session 3:		
Interventions:		
Notes:		
Homework:		
Session 4:		
Note to leader: Remind members that there are four sessions left.		
Interventions:		
Notes:		
Homework:		

(Continued)

(Continued)

Session 5:

Interventions:

Notes:

Homework:

Session 6:

Interventions:

Notes:

Homework:

Session 7:

Note to leader: Remind
members that there is one
session left. Assign
homework to integrate
what has been learned.

Interventions:

Notes:

Homework:

| **Session 8:** | Ending | Ending |

Interventions:

Notes:

Appendix D_____

Grid for Choosing Sessions Based on Current Research and Practice

Goals for Group Based on Literature and Counseling Practice	Interventions Suggested in the Literature to Address This Goal	Sessions Designed by
(List goal and reference and date; indicate cognitive, behavioral, or affective)	(Describe and list reference and date)	(List reference, date, page number)

Now examine your grid: What goals have interventions and sessions designed for them? For those that do not have full sessions designed for them, these are the sessions you need to design complete with goals, activities, and processing questions. The idea is not to reinvent the wheel here but to see what is already out there and then add to the literature with new group sessions for this type of group.

References _____

Abram, J. (2008). Identifying your family role. In L. J. Foss, J. Green, K. Wolfe-Stiltner, & J. L. DeLucia-Waack (Eds.), *School counselors share their favorite group activities: A guide to choosing, planning, conducting, and processing* (pp. 133–137). Alexandria, VA: Association for Specialists in Group Work.

Abraham, P., Lepisto, B., & Schultz, L. (1995). Adolescents' perception of process and specialty group therapy. *Psychotherapy, 32,* 70–76. doi:10.1037/0033-3204 .32.1.70

Akos, P., Hamm, J. V., Mack, S. G., & Dunaway, M. (2007). Utilizing the developmental influence of peers in middle school groups. *Journal for Specialists in Group Work, 32,* 51–60. doi:10.1080/01933920600977648

American Group Psychotherapy Association. (2007). *Practice guidelines for group psychotherapy: A cross-theoretical guide to developing and leading psychotherapy groups.* New York: Author. Retrieved from http://agpa.org/guidelines/index .html

Arkowitz, H. (1992). Integrative theories of therapy. In D. K. Freedheim (Ed.), *History of psychotherapy: A century of change.* Washington, DC: American Psychological Association.

Association for the Advancement of Social Work with Groups. (2005). *Standards for social work practice with groups* (2nd ed.). Alexandria, VA: Author. Retrieved from http://www.aaswg.org/standards-social-work-practice-with-groups

Barlow, S. H., Burlingame, G. M., & Fuhriman, A. (2000). Therapeutic applications of groups: From Pratt's "thought control classes" to modern group psychotherapy. *Group Dynamics: Theory, Research, and Practice, 4,* 115–134. doi:10.1037/ 1089-2699.4.1.115

Bauman, S., & Steen, S. (2009). Hurting and healing. In C. F. Salazar (Ed.), *Group work experts share their favorite multicultural activities: A guide to diversity-competent choosing, planning, conducting and processing* (pp. 79–82). Alexandria, VA: American Counseling Association.

Bauman, S., & Steen, S. (Producers). (2010). *Group counseling with children: A multicultural approach* [DVD]. Alexandria, VA: Association for Specialists in Group Work.

Bauman, S., & Steen, S. (Producers). (2012). *Group counseling with adolescents: A multicultural approach* [DVD]. Alexandria, VA: Association for Specialists in Group Work.

Becerra, M. (2009). Elephant in the room. In C. F. Salazar (Ed.), *Group work experts share their favorite multicultural activities: A guide to diversity-competent choosing, planning, conducting and processing* (p. 58). Alexandria, VA: American Counseling Association.

Beech Acres Airing Institute. (1993). *The boys and girls of group: Divorce and step-families* (4th ed.). Cincinnati, OH: Author.

Bond, G. R., Drake, R. E., & Becker, D. R. (2010). Beyond evidence-based practice: Nine ideal features of a mental health intervention. *Research on Social Work Practice, 20,* 493–501. doi:10.1177/1049731509358085

Bridbord, K. (2006). Autobiography. In J. L. DeLucia-Waack, K. Bridbord, J. Kleiner, & A. Nitza (Eds.), *Group work experts share their favorite activities: A guide to choosing, planning, conducting, and processing* (Rev. ed., pp. 28–29). Alexandria, VA: Association for Specialists in Group Work.

Bridbord, K., & DeLucia-Waack, J. (2011). Personality, leadership style, and theoretical orientation as predictors of group co-leadership satisfaction. *Journal for Specialists in Group Work, 36,* 202–221. doi:10.1080/01933922.2011.578 117

Bridbord, K., & Nitza, A. (2008). Processing activities to facilitate the transfer of learning outside of group. In L. L. Foss, J. Green, K. Wolfe-Stiltner, & J. DeLucia-Waack (Eds.), *School counselors share their favorite group activities: A guide to choosing, planning, conducting, and processing* (pp. 23–32). Alexandria, VA: Association for Specialists in Group Work.

Brown, B. (2006). Looking at process. In J. L. DeLucia-Waack, K. Bridbord, J. Kleiner, & A. Nitza (Eds.), *Group work experts share their favorite activities: A guide to choosing, planning, conducting, and processing* (Rev. ed., pp. 30–32). Alexandria, VA: Association for Specialists in Group Work.

Brown, N. (2006). A group image. In J. DeLucia-Waack, K. Bridbord, J. Kleiner, & A. Nitza (Eds.), *Group work experts share their favorite activities* (63–65). Alexandria, VA: ASGW.

Burlingame, G. M., Cox, J. C., Davies, D. R., Layne, C. M., & Gleave, R. (2011). The Group Selection Questionnaire: Further refinements in group member selection. *Group Dynamics: Theory, Research, and Practice, 15,* 60–74. doi:10.1037/a0020220

Burlingame, G. M., Fuhriman, A., & Johnson, J. E. (2002). Cohesion in group psychotherapy. In J. Norcross (Ed.), *Psychotherapy relationships that work: Therapist contributions and responsiveness to patients* (pp. 71–88). New York: Oxford University Press.

Burlingame, G., Fuhriman, A., & Mosier, J. (2003). The differential effectiveness of group psychotherapy: A meta-analytic perspective. *Group Dynamics: Theory, Research and Practice, 7,* 3–12. doi:10.1037/1089-2699.7.1.3

Burlingame, G., Strauss, B., Joyce, A., MacKenzie, K., Ogrodniczuk, J., & Taylor, S. (2006). *CORE battery: A revision and update.* New York: American Group Psychotherapy Association.

Burlingame, G., Davies, D., Cox, D., Baker, E., Pearson, M., Beecher, M. & Gleave, R. (2012). *The Group Readiness Questionnaire Manual.* Salt Lake City, Utah: OQ Measures.

Burlingame, G., Whitcomb, K., & Woodland, S. (2013). Process and outcome in group counseling and psychotherapy: A perspective. In J. DeLucia-Waack, C. R. Kalodner, & M. T. Riva (Eds.), *Handbook of group counseling and psychotherapy* (2nd ed.). Thousand Oaks, CA: Sage.

Campbell, A. (2008). Are you growing worries? In L. J. Foss, J. Green, K. Wolfe-Stiltner, & J. L. DeLucia-Waack (Eds.), *School counselors share their favorite group activities: A guide to choosing, planning, conducting, and processing* (p. 54). Alexandria, VA: Association for Specialists in Group Work.

Carrell, S. (2000). *Group exercises for adolescents: A manual for therapists* (2nd ed.). Thousand Oaks, CA: Sage.

Carter, E. F., Mitchell, S. L., & Krautheim, M. D. (2001). Understanding and addressing clients' resistance to group counseling. *Journal for Specialists in Group Work, 26*, 66–80. doi:10.1080/01933920108413778

Chapman, C. L., Baker, E. L., Porter, G., Thayer, S. D., & Burlingame, G. M. (2010). Rating group therapist interventions: The validation of the Group Psychotherapy Intervention Rating Scale. *Group Dynamics: Theory, Research, and Practice, 14*(1), 15–31.

Chen, M., & Rybak, C. J. (2004). *Group leadership skills: Interpersonal process in group counseling and therapy.* Pacific Grove, CA: Brooks/Cole.

Conyne, R. K. (1999). *Failures in group work: How we can learn from our mistakes.* Thousand Oaks, CA: Sage.

Conyne, R. (2009). What to look for in groups: Using the group multicultural sensitizer activity. In C. F. Salazar (Ed.), *Group work experts share their favorite multicultural activities: A guide to diversity-competent choosing, planning, conducting and processing* (pp. 239–247). Alexandria, VA: Association for Specialists in Group Work.

Conyne, R. (2003). Best practices in leading prevention groups. *Group Work Practice Ideas: Association for Specialists in Group Work, 32*, 9–12.

Corey, M. S., Corey, G., & Corey, C. (2010). *Groups: Process and practice* (8th ed.). Belmont, CA: Brooks/Cole.

Coventry, J. (2008). Risk bag. In L. L. Foss, J. Green, K. Wolfe-Stiltner, & J. DeLucia-Waack (Eds.), *School counselors share their favorite group activities: A guide to choosing, planning, conducting, and processing* (pp. 103–105). Alexandria, VA: Association for Specialists in Group Work.

Crespi, T. D., Gustafson, A. L., & Borges, S. M. (2005). Group counseling in the schools: Considerations for child and family issues. *Journal of Applied School Psychology, 22*(1), 2005. 67–85.

D'Andrea, M., & Daniels, J. (2009). Strategies to prevent cultural–racial prejudice. In C. F. Salazar (Ed.), *Group work experts share their favorite multicultural activities: A guide to diversity-competent choosing, planning, conducting and processing* (pp. 129–131). Alexandria, VA: Association for Specialists in Group Work.

Darst, K. V., & Funke, M. (2006). Stress Jenga. In J. L. DeLucia-Waack, K. H. Bridbord, J. S. Kleiner, & A. Nitza (Eds.), *Group work experts share their favorite activities: A guide to choosing, planning, conducting, and processing* (Rev. ed., pp. 37–38). Alexandria, VA: Association for Specialists in Group Work.

Day, S. X. (2013). A unifying theory for group and psychotherapy. In J. DeLucia-Waack, C. R. Kalodner, & M. T. Riva (Eds.), *Handbook of group counseling and psychotherapy* (2nd ed.). Thousand Oaks, CA: Sage.

DeLucia-Waack, J. L. (2001). *Using music in children of divorce groups: A session-by-session manual for counselors.* Alexandria, VA: American Counseling Association.

DeLucia-Waack, J. L. (2002). A written guide for planning and processing group sessions in anticipation of supervision. *Journal for Specialists in Group Work, 27*, 341–357. doi:10.1080/714860198

DeLucia-Waack, J. L. (2006). *Leading psychoeducational groups for children and adolescents.* Thousand Oaks, CA: Sage.

DeLucia-Waack, J. L., Bridbord, K. H., Kleiner, J. S., & Nitza, A. (Eds.). (2006). *Group work experts share their favorite activities: A guide to choosing, planning, conducting, and processing* (Rev. ed.). Alexandria, VA: Association for Specialists in Group Work.

DeLucia-Waack, J. L., & Donigian, J. (2004). *The practice of multicultural group work: Visions and perspectives from the field.* Pacific Grove, CA: Wadsworth Press.

DeLucia-Waack, J. L., & Fauth, J. (2004). Effective supervision of group leaders: Current theory, research, and implications for practice. In J. L. DeLucia-Waack, D. Gerrity, C. R. Kalodner, & M. Riva (Eds.), *Handbook of group counseling and psychotherapy* (pp. 136–151). Thousand Oaks, CA: Sage.

DeLucia-Waack, J. (2006). Closing: Thanking Others. In J. DeLucia-Waack, K. Bridbord, J. Kleiner, & A. Nitza (Eds.), *Group work experts share their favorite activities* (159–161). Alexandria, VA: ASGW.

DeLucia-Waack, J. (2006). Closing: What Have We Learned About Others. In J. DeLucia-Waack, K. Bridbord, J. Kleiner, & A Nitza (Eds.), *Group work experts share their favorite activities* (156–158). Alexandria, VA: ASGW.

DeLucia-Waack, J. L., Kalodner, C., & Riva, M. (Eds.). (2013). *Handbook of group counseling and psychotherapy* (2nd ed.). Thousand Oaks, CA: Sage.

DeLucia-Waack, J. L., & Nitza, A. (2010). Leading task groups in the schools. In B. T. Erford (Ed.), *Groups in the schools* (pp. 189–206). Columbus, OH: Pearson/Merrill/Prentice Hall.

DeLucia-Waack, J. L., & Nitza, A. (2011). Leading task groups. In B. T. Erford (Ed.), *Group work: Processes and applications* (pp. 171–186). Boston: Pearson/ Merrill/Prentice Hall.

DeLucia-Waack, J. (2011). Children of divorce groups. In G. Greif & P. Ephross (Eds.), *Group work with at-risk populations* (3rd ed., 93–114). New York: Oxford University Press.

DeLucia-Waack, J., Segrist, A., & Horne, A. (Producers). (2008). *Leading groups with adolescents* [DVD]. Alexandria, VA: Association for Specialists in Group Work.

Dies, R. R. (1994). Therapist variables in group psychology research. In A. Fuhriman & G. M. Burlingame (Eds.), *Handbook of group psychotherapy: An empirical and clinical synthesis* (pp. 113–154). New York: Wiley.

Doughty, L. (2006). Guess who? In J. L. DeLucia-Waack, K. Bridbord, J. Kleiner, & A. Nitza (Eds.), *Group work experts share their favorite activities: A guide to choosing, planning, conducting, and processing* (Rev. ed., pp. 39–40). Alexandria, VA: Association for Specialists in Group Work.

Dugo, J. M., & Beck, A. P. (1997). Significance and complexity of early phases in the development of the co-therapy relationship. *Group Dynamics: Theory, Research, and Practice, 1,* 294–305. doi:10.1037/1089-2699.1.4.294

Dye. H. A. (2006). Previewing. In J. DeLucia-Waack, K. Bridbord, J. Kleiner, & A. Nitza (Eds.), *Group work experts share their favorite activities* (177 –180). Alexandria, VA: ASGW.

Erguner-Tekinalp, B. (2008). Millions of families. In L. J. Foss, J. Green, K. Wolfe-Stiltner, & J. L. DeLucia-Waack (Eds.), *School counselors share their favorite group activities: A guide to choosing, planning, conducting, and processing* (pp. 58–61). Alexandria, VA: Association for Specialists in Group Work.

Erguner-Tekinalp, B. (2008). We live under the same sky. In L. Foss, J. Green, K. Wolfe-stiltner, & J. DeLucia-Waack (Eds.), *School Counselors share their favorite group activities* (77–78). Alexandria, VA: ASGW.

Fleckenstein, L. B., & Horne, A. M. (2004). Anger management groups. In J. DeLucia-Waack, D. A. Gerrity, C. R. Kalodner, & M. T. Riva (Eds.), *Handbook of group counseling and psychotherapy* (547–562). Thousand Oaks, CA: Sage.

Foss, L., Green, J., Wolfe-Stiltner, K., & DeLucia-Waack, J. L. (Eds.). (2008). *School counselors share their share their favorite group activities: A guide to choosing, planning, conducting, and processing.* Alexandria, VA: Association for Specialists in Group Work.

Gazda, G. (1989). *Group counseling: A developmental approach* (4th ed.). Boston: Allyn & Bacon.

Gerrity, D. (2006). Our two faces. In J. L. DeLucia-Waack, K. Bridbord, J. Kleiner, & A. Nitza (Eds.), *Group work experts share their favorite activities: A guide to choosing, planning, conducting, and processing* (Rev. ed., pp. 120–121). Alexandria, VA: Association for Specialists in Group Work.

Gladding, S. T. (2003). *Group work: A counseling specialty* (2nd ed.). Englewood Cliffs, NJ: Merrill.

Griner, D., & Smith, T. B. (2006). Culturally adapted mental health intervention: A meta-analytic review. *Psychotherapy: Theory, Research, Practice, Training, 43,* 531–548. doi:10.1037/0033-3204.43.4.531

Henriksen, R., & Paladino, D. A. (2009b). My multiple heritage identity. In C. F. Salazar (Ed.), *Group work experts share their favorite multicultural activities: A guide to diversity-competent choosing, planning, conducting and processing* (pp. 202–205). Alexandria, VA: Association for Specialists in Group Work.

Hines, P. L., & Fields, T. H. (2002). Pregroup screening issues for school counselors. *Journal for Specialists in Group Work, 27,* 358–376. doi:10.1080/714860199

Hoag, M. J., & Burlingame, G. M. (1997). Evaluating the effectiveness of child and adolescent group treatment: A meta-analytic review. *Journal of Clinical Child Psychology, 26*(3), 234–246.

Horne, A. (2006). Fiddler on the roof. In J. L. DeLucia-Waack, K. Bridbord, J. Kleiner, & A. Nitza (Eds.), *Group work experts share their favorite activities: A guide to choosing, planning, conducting, and processing* (Rev. ed., pp. 125–126). Alexandria, VA: Association for Specialists in Group Work.

Horowitz, L. M., Alden, L. E., Wiggins, J. S., & Pincus, A. L. (2000). *Inventory of Interpersonal Problems manual.* Tampa, FL: Psychological Corporation.

Horvath, A., & Greenberg, L. (1989). Development and validation of the Working Alliance Inventory. *Journal of Counseling Psychology, 52,* 310–321. doi:10.1037/00220167.36.2.223

Hulse-Killacky, D., Killacky, J., & Donigian, J. (2001). *Making task groups work in your world.* Upper Saddle River, NJ: Prentice Hall.

Jackson, A. P. (2009). Level playing field. In C. F. Salazar (Ed.), *Group work experts share their favorite multicultural activities: A guide to diversity-competent choosing, planning, conducting and processing* (pp. 62–65). Alexandria, VA: American Counseling Association.

Jacobs, E., & Schimmel, C. (2009). Processing activities to facilitate the transfer of learning outside the group. In C. Salazar (Ed.), *Group work experts share their favorite multicultural activities: A guide to diversity-competent choosing, planning, conducting, and processing* (pp. 135–145). Alexandria, VA: Association for Specialists in Group Work.

Johnson, J. E. (2008). Using research-supported group treatments. *Journal of Counseling Psychology, 64,* 1206–1224. doi:10.1002/jclp.20532

Jones, K. D., & Robinson, E. H., III. (2000). Psychoeducational groups: A model for choosing topics and exercises appropriate to group stage. *Journal for Specialists in Group Work, 25,* 356–365. doi:10.1080/01933920008411679

Kalter, N. (1998). Group interventions for children of divorce. In K. C. Stoiber & T. R. Kratochwill (Eds.), *Handbook of group intervention for children and families* (pp. 120–140). Boston: Allyn & Bacon.

Karcher, E. (2008). Up, up, and away. In L. J. Foss, J. Green, K. Wolfe-Stiltner, & J. L. DeLucia-Waack (Eds.), *School counselors share their favorite group activities: A guide to choosing, planning, conducting, and processing* (p. 123). Alexandria, VA: Association for Specialists in Group Work.

Kivlighan, D. M., Jr., & Goldfine, D. C. (1991). Endorsement of therapeutic factors as a function of stage of group development and participant interpersonal attitudes. *Journal of Counseling Psychology, 38,* 150–158. doi:10.1037/0022-0167.38.2.150

Kovacs, M. (1992). *The Children's Depression Inventory manual.* North Tonawanda, NY: Multi-Health Systems.

Kurdek, L., & Berg, B. (1987). Children's Beliefs About Parental Divorce Scale: Psychometric characteristics and concurrent validity. *Journal of Consulting and Clinical Psychology, 55,* 712–718. doi:10.1037/0022-006X.55.5.712

Leary, T. F. (1957). *Interpersonal diagnosis of personality.* New York: Ronald Press.

Leddick, G. R. (2006). You're one unique cookie. In C. F. Salazar (Ed.), *Group work experts share their favorite multicultural activities: A guide to diversity-competent choosing, planning, conducting and processing* (pp. 150–152). Alexandria, VA: Association for Specialists in Group Work.

LeGrand, K. (2006). The kid's grief kit. In J. L. DeLucia-Waack, K. Bridbord, J. Kleiner, & A. Nitza (Eds.), *Group work experts share their favorite activities: A guide to choosing, planning, conducting, and processing* (Rev. ed., pp. 133–134). Alexandria, VA: Association for Specialists in Group Work.

Levy, L. B., & O'Hara, M. W. (2010). Psychotherapeutic interventions for depressed, low-income women: A review of the literature. *Clinical Psychology Review, 30,* 934–950. doi:10.1016/j.cpr.2010.06.006

Lieberman, M. A., Yalom, I. D., & Miles, M. B. (1973). *Encounter groups: First facts.* New York: Basic Books.

Luke, M. (2013). Effective group leader skills. In J. DeLucia-Waack, C. R. Kalodner, & M. T. Riva (Eds.), *Handbook of group counseling and psychotherapy* (2nd ed.). Thousand Oaks, CA: Sage.

MacGowan, M. J., & Hanbidge, A. S. (2013). Advancing evidence-based group work in community mental health settings: Methods, challenges and opportunities. In J. DeLucia-Waack, C. R. Kalodner, & M. T. Riva (Eds.), *Handbook of group counseling and psychotherapy* (2nd ed.). Thousand Oaks, CA: Sage.

MacKenzie, K. R. (1983). The clinical application of group climate measure. In R. R. Dies & K. MacKenzie (Eds.), *Advances in group psychotherapy:*

Integrating research and practice (pp. 159–170). New York: International Universities Press.

Manning, N. (2005). Does the Therapeutic Community Work? The Politics of Knowledge. *Therapeutic Communities, 26*(4), 385–389.

Martin, A., Rief, W., Klaiberg, A., & Braehler, E. (2006). Validity of the Brief Patient Health Questionnaire Mood Scale (PHQ-9) in the general population. *General Hospital Psychiatry, 28*, 71–77. doi:10.1016/j.genhosppsych.2005.07.003

McDermut, W., Miller, I. W., Brown, R. A. (2001). The efficacy of group psychotherapy for depression: A meta-analysis and review of the empirical research. *Clinical Psychology: Science and Practice, 8*(1), 98–116.

Merchant, N. (2009). Types of diversity-related groups. In C. F. Salazar (Ed.), *Group work experts share their favorite multicultural activities: A guide to diversity-competent choosing, planning, conducting and processing* (pp. 13–24). Alexandria, VA: Association for Specialists in Group Work.

Morganett, R. S. (1990). *Skills for living: Group counseling for young adolescents.* Champaign, IL: Research Press.

Morganett, R. S. (1994). *Skills for living: Group counseling for elementary school students.* Champaign, IL: Research Press.

Morran, D. K., Stockton, R., Cline, R. J., & Teed, C. (1998). Facilitating feedback exchange in groups: Leader interventions. *Journal for Specialists in Group Work, 23*, 257–268. doi:10.1080/01933929808411399

Morran, D. K., Stockton, R., & Harris, M. (1991). Analysis of group leader and member feedback messages. *Journal of Group Psychotherapy, Psychodrama, and Sociometry, 44*, 126–135.

Morgan, Robert D. (2004). Groups With Offenders and Mandated Clients. In J. DeLucia-Waack, D. A. Gerrity, C. R. Kalodner, & M. T. Riva (Eds.), *Handbook of group counseling and psychotherapy* (388–400). Thousand Oaks, CA: Sage Publications.

Morran, D. K., Stockton, R., & Whittingham, M. H. (2004). Effective leader interventions for counseling and psychotherapy groups. In J. L. DeLucia-Waack, D. A. Gerrity, C. R. Kalodner, & M. T. Riva (Eds.), *Handbook of group counseling and psychotherapy* (pp. 91–103). Thousand Oaks, CA: Sage.

Muñoz, R. F., Ippen, C. G., Rao, S., Le, H.-N., & Dwyer, E. V. (2000). *Manual for group cognitive-behavioral therapy of major depression: A reality management approach.* Retrieved from http://medschool2.ucsf.edu/latino/pdf/CBTDEN/overview.pdf

Muñoz, R. F., & Mendelson, T. (2005). Toward evidence-based interventions for diverse populations: The San Francisco General Hospital prevention and treatment manuals. *Journal of Consulting and Clinical Psychology, 73*(5), 790–799.

Muñoz, R. F., & Miranda, J. (1986). *Group therapy manual for cognitive-behavioral treatment of depression.* Unpublished manual, San Francisco General Hospital Depression Clinic.

Payne, K. T., & Marcus, D. K. (2008). The efficacy of group psychotherapy for older adult clients: A meta-analysis. *Group Dynamics: Theory, Research, and Practice, 12*, 267–278. doi:10.1037/a0013519

Pedro-Carroll, J. L. , & Cowen , E. L. (1985). The Children of Divorce Intervention project: An investigation of the efficacy of a school-based prevention program. *Journal of Consulting and Clinical Psychology, 53*, 603 – 611 .

Pfeiffer, J. W., & Jones, J. E. (1973). Co-facilitating. In J. W. Pfeiffer & J. E. Jones (Eds.). *The 1975 annual handbook for group facilitation* (219–225). Iowa City, IA: University Associates.

Piper, W. E., Ogrodniczuk, J. S., Joyce, A., & Weideman, R. (2011). *Short-term group therapies for complicated grief.* Washington, DC: American Psychological Association.

Rapin, L. S., & Keel, L. P. (1998). ASGW best practice guidelines. *Journal for Specialists in Group Work, 23,* 237–244.

Reynolds, C. R., & Richmond, B. O. (1985). *Revised Children's Manifest Anxiety Scale.* Los Angeles: Western Psychological Services.

Riva, M. T. (2013). Supervision of group leaders. In J. DeLucia-Waack, C. R. Kalodner, & M. T. Riva (Eds.), *Handbook of group counseling and psychotherapy* (2nd ed.). Thousand Oaks, CA: Sage.

Riva, M. T., Wachtel, T., & Lasky, G. (2004). Effective leadership in group counseling and psychotherapy: Research and practice. In J. DeLucia-Waack, D. Gerrity, C. Kalodner, & M. Riva (Eds.), *Handbook of group counseling and psychotherapy* (pp. 37–48). Thousand Oaks, CA: Sage.

Rotsinger-Stemen, S., & Whittingham, M. (2013). *Focused Brief Group Therapy: An effectiveness study.* Honolulu, HI:Poster Presentation at APA National Convention.

Rubel, D. J., & Kline, W. B. (2008). An exploratory study of expert group leadership. *Journal for Specialists in Group Work, 33,* 138–160. doi:10.1080/019339 20801977363

Salazar, C. F. (Ed.). (2009). *Group work experts share their favorite multicultural activities: A guide to diversity-competent choosing, planning, conducting and processing.* Alexandria: VA: Association for Specialists in Group Work.

Shapiro, E. (1999). Cotherapy. In J. R. Price & D. R. Hescheles (Eds.), *A guide to starting psychotherapy groups* (pp. 53–61). San Diego: Academic Press.

Shulman, L. (2011). *Dynamics and skills of group counseling.* Belmont, CA: Brooks/Cole, Cengage Learning.

Singh, A. A., Merchant, N., Skudrzyk, B., & Ingene, D. (2012). *Association for Specialists in Group Work: Multicultural and social justice competence principles for group workers.* Retrieved from http://www.asgw.org/pdf/ASGW_MC_SJ_Priniciples_Final_ASGW.pdf

Slocum, Y. S. (1987). A survey of expectations about group therapy among clinical and non-clinical populations. *International Journal of Group Psychotherapy, 37,* 39–54. doi:10.1080/01933929808411399

Smead, R. (1995). *Skills and techniques for group work with children and adolescents.* Champaign, IL: Research Press.

Smead, R. (Presenter). (1996). *Skills and techniques for group counseling with youth* [Video]. Champaign, IL: Research Press.

Smith, T. B., Rodríguez, M. D., & Bernal, G. (2011). Culture. *Journal of Clinical Psychology, 67,* 166–175.

Sommers-Flanagan, R., Barrett-Hakanson, T., Clarke, C., & Sommers-Flanagan, J. (2000). A psychoeducational school-based coping and social skills group for depressed students. *Journal for Specialists in Group Work, 25,* 170–190.

Stacciarini, J. M., O'Keeffe, M., & Mathews, M. (2007). Group therapy as treatment for depressed Latino women: A review of the literature. *Issues in Mental Health Nursing, 28,* 473–488. doi:10.1080/01612840701344431

Steen, S. (2011). Academic and personal development through group work: An exploratory study. *Journal for Specialists in Group Work, 36,* 129–143. doi:10.1080/01933922.2011.562747

Stolberg, A. L., & Cullen, P. M. (1983). Preventive psychopathology in children of divorce: The divorce adjustment process. In L. Kurdek (Ed.), *New directions for child development: Children and divorce* (71–81). San Francisco: Jossey-Bass.

Stockton, R., Morran, D. K., & Nitza, A. G. (2000). Processing group events: A conceptual map for leaders. *Journal for Specialists in Group Work, 25,* 343–355. doi:10.1080/01933920008411678

Subich, L. M., & Coursol, D. H. (1985). Counseling expectations of clients and non-clients for group and individual treatment modes. *Journal of Counseling Psychology, 32*(2), 245–251.

Thomas, M. C. (2006). Who taught you how to love? In J. L. DeLucia-Waack, K. Bridbord, J. Kleiner, & A. Nitza (Eds.), *Group work experts share their favorite activities: A guide to choosing, planning, conducting, and processing (Rev.)* (pp. 166–169). Alexandria, VA: Association for Specialists in Group Work.

Thomas, R. V., & Pender, D. A. (2008). *Association for Specialists in Group Work: Best practice guidelines 2007 revisions.* Retrieved from http://asgw.org/pdf/Best_Practices.pdf

Toseland, R. W., & Siporin, M. (1986). Response to critiques by George Gazda, and K. Roy Mackenzie. *International Journal of Group Psychotherapy, 36*(3), 483–485.

Toseland, R. W., & Siporin, M. (1986). When to recommend group treatment: A review of the clinical and the research literature. *International Journal of Group Psychotherapy, 36*(2), 171–201.

Tyson, L. E., Perusse, R., & Whitledge, J. (2004). *Critical incidents in group counseling.* Alexandria, VA: American Counseling Association.

Villalba, J. A. (2007). Incorporating wellness into group work in elementary schools. *Journal for Specialists in Group Work, 32,* 31–40. doi:10.1080/01933920600977556

Vogel, D. L., Shechtman, Z., & Wade, N. G. (2010). The role of public and self-stigma in predicting attitudes toward group counseling. *The Counseling Psychologist, 38,* 904–922. doi:10.1177/0011000010368297

Ward, D. E. (2013). Effective processing in groups. In J. DeLucia-Waack, C. R. Kalodner, & M. T. Riva (Eds.), *Handbook of group counseling and psychotherapy* (2nd ed.). Thousand Oaks, CA: Sage.

Wells, M. G., Burlingame, G. M., Lambert, M. J., & Hope, C. A. (1996). Conceptualization and measurement of patient change during psychotherapy: Development of the Outcome Questionnaire and Youth Outcome Questionnaire. *Psychotherapy: Theory, Research, Practice, and Training, 33,* 275–283.

Whittingham, M. (November, 2012). *Focused Brief Group Therapy: A Practice Based Evidence Approach.* Distance learning course/Teleconference. AGPA Distance Based Learning Workshop.

Whittingham, M., & Lotz, J. (2012). *Focused Brief Group Therapy Treatment Manual.* Unpublished manuscript.

Wile, D. B., Bron, G. D., & Pollack, H. B. (1970). The group therapy questionnaire: An instrument for study of leadership in small groups. *Psychological Reports, 27*(1), 263–273.

Wilson, F. R. (2006). Feedback as poetry. In J. L. DeLucia-Waack, K. H. Bridbord, J. S. Kleiner, & A. Nitza (Eds.), *Group work experts share their favorite activities: A guide to choosing, planning, conducting, and processing* (Rev. ed., p. 165). Alexandria, VA: Association for Specialists in Group Work.

Wilson, F. R., Rapin, L. S., & Haley-Banez, L. (2000). *Professional standards for the training of group workers.* Retrieved from http://asgw.org/pdf/training _standards.pdf

Whittingham, M. (2013). Group work in colleges and university counseling centers. In J. L. Delucia-Waack, C. R. Kalodner, & M. T. Riva (Eds.), *Handbook of group counseling and psychotherapy* (2nd ed.). Thousand Oaks, CA: Sage.

Yalom, I. D. (1995). *The theory and practice of group psychotherapy* (4th ed.). New York: Basic Books.

Yalom, I. D. (with Leszcz, M.). (2005). *The theory and practice of group psychotherapy* (5th ed.). New York: Basic Books.

Index _____

About the Authors _____

Janice L. DeLucia-Waack is currently an associate professor and program director for school counseling in the Department of Counseling, School, and Educational Psychology at the University at Buffalo, State University of New York. She is the former editor of *The Journal for Specialists in Group Work* and is a fellow of the Association for Specialists in Group Work division of the American Counseling Association and of Group Psychology and Group Psychotherapy, Division 49 of the American Psychological Association. She is author/editor of two books, *Using Music in Children of Divorce Groups: A Session-by-Session Manual for Counselors* and *Multicultural Counseling and Training: Implications and Challenges for Practice*, and coeditor/author of three other books: *Handbook of Group Counseling and Psychotherapy* (2nd edition, with Cynthia Kalodner and Maria Riva), *The Practice of Multicultural Group Work: Visions and Perspectives From the Field* (with Jeremiah Donigian), and *Group Work Experts Share Their Favorite Activities: A Guide to Choosing, Planning, Conducting, and Processing* (with Karen Bridbord and Jennifer Kleiner). She received a bachelor's degree in psychology from Eisenhower College, a master's degree in family studies from the University of Maryland, and a PhD in counseling psychology from the Pennsylvania State University.

Amy Nitza is currently an associate professor and director of counselor education in the College of Education and Public Policy at Indiana University-Purdue University Fort Wayne (IPFW). She was a Fulbright Scholar at the University of Botswana, where she studied the relationship of cultural factors and group dynamics and developed a group intervention for adolescent girls. She is a past secretary and newsletter editor of the Association for Specialists in Group Work. She is the producer of the DVD *Leading Groups with Adolescents* (featuring Janice L. DeLucia-Waack, Al Segrist, and Arthur Horne) and author of the DVD study guide. She is also the author/coauthor of several journal articles and book chapters on group work. She is the coeditor of the forthcoming book: *Group Workers Share Their Favorite Activities, Volume II: A Practical Handbook for Beginning and Advanced Group Leaders*. She received a bachelor's degree in psychology and a master's degree in mental health counseling from Purdue University, and a PhD in counseling psychology from Indiana University.

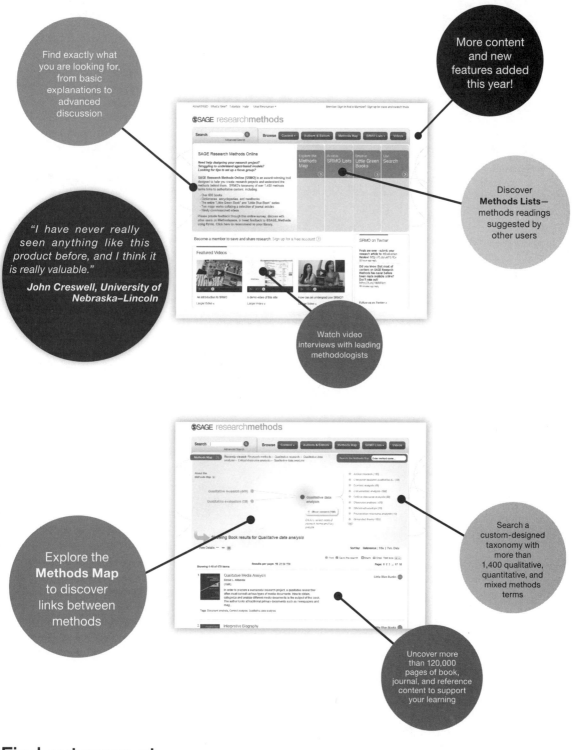

⑤SAGE research**methods**

The essential online tool for researchers from the world's leading methods publisher

Find exactly what you are looking for, from basic explanations to advanced discussion

More content and new features added this year!

"I have never really seen anything like this product before, and I think it is really valuable."
John Creswell, University of Nebraska–Lincoln

Discover **Methods Lists**— methods readings suggested by other users

Watch video interviews with leading methodologists

Explore the **Methods Map** to discover links between methods

Search a custom-designed taxonomy with more than 1,400 qualitative, quantitative, and mixed methods terms

Uncover more than 120,000 pages of book, journal, and reference content to support your learning

Find out more at
www.sageresearchmethods.com